Going Hog Wild
with

Country Cooking

COLLECTED AND COMPILED
BY
SUSIE CONNELL BROWN AND VICKI CONNELL SPECK
P. O. BOX 1371
TEXARKANA, ARKANSAS 75504

Your Razorback Country Cooking Cookbook may be obtained from
Razorback Country Cooking
P. O. Box 1371
Texarkana, Arkansas 75504

Order Blanks in back of book
$10.95 per copy $1.50 postage and handling

First Printing June 1986 5,000 Copies

"Susie Connell Brown or Vicki Connell Speck have no reason to doubt that recipe ingredients, instructions, and directions will work successfully. However, the ingredients, instructions, and directions have not necessarily been thoroughly or systematically tested, and the cook should not hesitate to test and question procedures and directions before preparation. The recipes in this book have been collected from various sources, and neither Susie Connell Brown nor Vicki Connell Speck nor any contributor, publisher, printer, distributor, or seller of this book is responsible for errors or omissions."

Printed in United States of America
by
Wimmer Brothers
P. O. Box 18408
Memphis, Tn. 38181-0408

International Standard Book Number-09616573-0-8

ACKNOWLEDGEMENTS

Cover Design and Art by Vicki Connell Speck and
Susie Connell Brown

DEDICATION

To our mother, Lolita Connell Mills, for her constant support and encouragement, and to Razorback Country Cooking fans everywhere.

"I'd walk a million miles for one of your smiles."

PIG TALE

For hundreds of years Razorbacks have been a part of history and a source of folklore and humor.

In the South, the Razorback traits were crossed with the domestic hog to produce one of the principal economic and social factors of the region. What he lacks in speed and strength, he makes up for in his ability to take punishment and bounce back.

I am reminded of the story of a country farmer who bought dynamite to clear stumps from his land. One of his hogs accidently came upon a stick of dynamite and ate it. After which, he wandered into the stall of the farmer's mule. He was kicked until the dynamite exploded. The following day the farmer was confronted by a neighbor who had heard the explosion and was asked what had happened. The farmer explained, that his barn was leveled, all the windows were broken out of his house, his mule was killed, and he had one very sick hog!.

It is with that stamina that this cookbook was begun. Just as surely as God made the Razorback, God made all of us to develop and use our talents to bring happiness to others. I sincerely hope that you will enjoy and use the RAZORBACK COUNTRY recipes in this book.

TABLE OF CONTENTS

Acknowledgements and Dedication 3

Pig Tale 4

Weights and Measurements 6

Appetizers and Hors d'oeuvres 7

Beverages 17

Breads 25

Cakes and Frostings 39

Candies and Cookies 59

Fish and Seafood 69

Fowl and Poultry 81

Fruits and Vegetables 99

Meats 113

Miscellaneous 129

      Eggs 131

      Other Desserts 133

      Pickles and Relishes 137

      Preserves 139

      Sauces and Spreads 140

      Snacks 142

Pastries and Pies 143

Penny Pinchin One Dish Meals 155

Salads and Salad Dressings 173

Dieting 186

Index 187

WEIGHTS AND MEASUREMENTS

Dash	1-4 drops	½ fluid ounce
3 teaspoons	1 tablespoon	2 fluid ounces
4 tablespoons	¼ cup	8 fluid ounces
16 tablespoons	1 cup (½ pint)	16 fluid ounces
2 cups	1 pint	32 fluid ounces
2 pints	1 quart	128 fluid ounces
4 quarts	1 gallon	⅛ cup
2 tablespoons	1 ounce	¼ cup
4 tablespoons	2 ounces	1 cup
16 tablespoons	8 ounces	1 pound
2 cups	16 ounces	

Appetizers
and
Hors d'oeuvres

ARKADELPHIA ARTICHOKE HORS D'OEUVRES

1 artichoke per person
Water
2 whole lemons

1 cup mayonnaise
¼ cup horseradish

Trim sharp points from tops of artichokes. Trim off stem so that it can sit on its "bottom". Place artichokes into boiling water that is seasoned with lemon juice from 1 lemon and squeezed lemon rind. Boil for 30 to 40 minutes until the meat of a leaf is tender when tested. Meanwhile, squeeze the juice from remaining lemon, add horseradish and mayonnaise. Mix well. Dip artichoke leaf bases into dip for a succulent delight. Don't forget to eat the artichoke heart, the best part!

FRIED CHEESE

Cheddar, Muenster or Colby
  cheese
2 eggs, beaten

Seasoned dry bread crumbs
Vegetable cooking oil

Cut cheese into cubes. Dip cubes in eggs. Coat each with bread crumbs. Fry in hot oil until slightly brown. Serve immediately.

GARLIC CHEESE BALL

½ pound processed American
  cheese spread
½ pound cream cheese
¼ pound shredded sharp
  Cheddar cheese

½ to 1 cup finely chopped
  pecans
Dash garlic powder or garlic
  salt

Let cheese and cream cheese get to room temperature. Shred Cheddar cheese. Mix all three cheeses together. Sprinkle a dash of garlic powder or salt in cheese and mix well with hands. Shape into two balls and roll in chopped pecans until covered. These freeze well for later use. You may also roll the balls in chili powder and mix the pecans in with the cheese. Serve with crackers.

PLAY BALL CHEESE BALL

One 8 ounce package cream
cheese
One 8 ounce package
processed cheese spread
One 8 ounce package Cheddar
cheese
One 8 ounce package blue
cheese

One 8 ounce jar of processed
cheese spread
3 tablespoons Worcestershire
sauce
2 teaspoons cayenne pepper
2 teaspoons garlic powder
Parsley flakes
Chili powder

Let cheeses stand at room temperature until soft. Mix with remaining ingredients and shape into balls. Roll in parsley flakes or chili powder. The yield is 3 large cheese balls.

AUNT OLIVE'S CHEESE PUFFS

¼ cup butter
½ cup all-purpose flour
½ teaspoon salt
½ teaspoon paprika

1 large jar stuffed green olives,
drained
One cup shredded American
cheese

Combine all ingredients and mix well. Cover each olive with a teaspoon of mixture. Form a ball. Place on a cookie sheet and bake at 400 degrees for 15 minutes. These can be made ahead of time, frozen and kept until ready for use.

EIGHT LAYERED PARTY DIP

2 or 3 small avocados or 2 cans
   frozen avocados
2 tablespoons lemon juice
½ teaspoon salt
¼ teaspoon pepper
11 drops tabasco
One 8 ounce carton sour cream
½ cup mayonnaise
One ½ package taco seasoning

Two 10½ ounce cans bean dip
1 cup chopped onion
2 or 3 chopped tomatoes
One 2¼ ounce can black olives,
   sliced
8 ounces shredded Cheddar
   cheese
One 9 ounce can picante sauce

Peel and mash avocados or use canned. Mix avocados with lemon juice, salt, pepper and tabasco. Set aside. Mix sour cream, mayonnaise, and taco seasoning. Set aside. In large bowl spread bean dip, picante sauce, avocado mixture, sour cream mixture, then layer with onions, tomatoes, black olives, and top with shredded cheese, great for after game parties served with chips.

HOT ARTICHOKE DIP

1 cup mayonnaise
1 cup Parmesan cheese
One 14 ounce can artichoke
   hearts

Dash of garlic powder

Drain and chop artichoke hearts. Combine with mayonnaise and cheese. Place in small casserole dish and bake at 350 degrees, for 20 to 25 minutes. Serve with crackers of your choice. The yield is 6 servings.

HOT BROCCOLI DIP

1 package frozen chopped
   broccoli
1 roll garlic cheese
1 roll nippy cheese
2 small onions, chopped

One 2½ ounce jar mushrooms
One 10¾ ounce can mushroom
   soup
½ cup chopped celery

Cook broccoli according to directions on package and drain. Melt cheeses, add broccoli and remaining ingredients. Serve hot.

SMACKOVER SHRIMP DIP

One 14 to 16 ounce package of precooked shrimp

One 10¾ ounce can cream of shrimp soup

One 6 ounce roll garlic flavored cheese

One 3 ounce can mushrooms, drained

2 tablespoons lemon juice

Mix all ingredients. Serve with crackers of your choice.

Make that extra point! Serve an appetizer.

GOAL POST SHRIMP DIP

One 4½ ounce can shrimp, drained and chopped
2 tablespoons milk
One 8 ounce package cream cheese or neufchatel cheese

2 teaspoons lemon juice
Dash of Worcestershire sauce

Combine softened cheese and milk. Mix until well blended. Add remaining ingredients and mix well. Serve with vegetable slices or your favorite chips. The yield is 1½ cups.

"TOMATO" DIP

Two 32 ounce cans tomatoes
1 can tomato paste
1 tablespoon monosodium glutamate
1 teaspoon oregano
½ teaspoon crushed red pepper

6 jalapeño peppers, chopped fine
2 onions, chopped
Two 4 ounce cans sliced mushrooms

Mix and simmer for 4 hours. Cool and serve with any type of chip or cracker.

VEGETABLE PATCH DIP

1 pint mayonnaise
1 pint sour cream
3 tablespoons minced fresh parsley or 1 tablespoon dried

3 tablespoons grated onion
3 tablespoons dill weed
1½ tablespoons seasoned salt

Mix all ingredients. Cover in tight container and refrigerate for several hours or overnight. Use any favorite raw vegetable such as carrots, broccoli, cauliflower, celery, turnips, or tomatoes. Hollow out a red cabbage and place dip in hollowed out shell. Place vegetables around cabbage on a tray. This makes a decorative center piece.

WILD DUCK DEWITT

2 wild ducks, (prepared as
PECKERWOOD WILD DUCK
IN RED WINE GRAVY)
1 package of long grain and
wild rice

Red wine gravy
Melba toast rounds

Prepare PECKERWOOD WILD DUCK IN RED WINE GRAVY. Remove meat from bones and cut into bite size pieces. Prepare rice as instructed on the package. Mix together ducks, rice, and red wine gravy. Serve with Melba toast rounds. Serves 12.

MOUNTAINBURG FROSTED GRAPES

Grapes, all sizes and kinds
Egg whites

Granulated sugar

Wash and dry grapes. Pull grapes apart into small bunches or clusters. Brush grapes with beaten egg whites and roll until coated in sugar. Place on rack to dry for 1 hour. They make easy hors d'oeuvres or serve at dinner with an assortment of cheeses.

DEVIL'S DEN HAM PUFFS

One 6¾ ounce can deviled ham
One 8 ounce package cream
cheese
One egg yolk
¼ teaspoon horseradish
¼ teaspoon salt

½ teaspoon onion juice
1 teaspoon baking powder
1 loaf thin sliced sandwich
bread
Paprika

Cut 1 inch diameter rounds of bread and toast on both sides. Mix all ingredients except deviled ham until smooth. Spread each toast round with deviled ham and then with the blended cheese mixture. Bake for 10 minutes at 375 degrees.

"Snout approved!"

LEMON MUSHROOMS

1½ pounds small mushrooms, fresh
1 medium lemon
¼ cup vegetable oil

2 tablespoons soy sauce
¼ teaspoon salt
¼ teaspoon sugar

Rinse mushrooms and trim stems. Cut lemon into 6 thin slices and squeeze juice from remaining piece. Heat mushrooms in oil. Stir in lemon slices, juice, soy sauce, salt and sugar. Cook for 5 minutes or until mushrooms are tender.

MAGNOLIA MARINATED MUSHROOMS, SHRIMP AND ARTICHOKES

2 pounds fresh cooked, peeled, deveined shrimp
One 8 ounce can of whole button mushrooms
Two 14 ounce cans tiny artichoke hearts
2 onions, sliced thinly in rings

3 packages salad dressing mix (1 blue cheese, 1 garlic, 1 Italian)
Salt to taste
One 2 ounce bottle capers, optional

Prepare packages of dressing according to directions on each package but omit water. Replace with red wine vinegar. Cover remaining ingredients with marinade overnight in refrigerator. Stir carefully. Serve with decorative toothpicks.

STUFFED MUSHROOM HOR D'OEUVRES

12 large mushrooms, fresh
6 small green onions
10 crushed crackers

½ cup Parmesan cheese, grated
3 tablespoons margarine

Remove and discard stems. Wash mushrooms. Mince green onions and combine with crackers and Parmesan cheese. Add softened margarine to mixture. Stuff mushrooms. Place in covered baking dish. Bake for 25 minutes in preheated oven at 350 degrees. The yield is 4 servings.

OYSTER HOR D'OEUVRES

1 pint oysters
12 slices bacon
½ teaspoon salt

⅛ teaspoon lemon pepper
⅛ teaspoon paprika
2 tablespoons chopped parsley

Drain oysters and lay each across a half a slice of bacon. Mix all seasonings together and sprinkle over oysters. Roll bacon around oyster and secure with a toothpick. Place oysters on a rack in a baking pan and bake in oven at 450 degrees for about 10 minutes or until bacon is crisp. Remove toothpicks before serving. The yield is 4 to 6 servings.

Beverages

BRINKLEY'S BRANDY ICE

4 ounces Brandy
2 ounces dark creme de cocoa
4-5 ice cubes

Vanilla ice cream
Nutmeg (for topping)

Frappe all ingredients in blender until smooth. Serve in long stemmed glasses. Top with a dash of nutmeg.

COZY COCOA MOCHA

⅓ cup sugar
¼ cup cocoa
2 teaspoons instant coffee
¼ teaspoon salt
2 whole cloves

¾ cup water
4½ cups milk
2 teaspoons vanilla
Cinnamon stick
Whipped cream (optional)

Mix cocoa, coffee, sugar, salt, cloves, and water in pan and bring to boil. Add milk and heat until steaming hot. Stir frequently. Add vanilla and cinnamon stick. Serve hot with whipped cream topping if desired. The yield is 8 servings.

"Put your feet up by the fire and watch the snow fall."

CRYSTAL SPRINGS COLADA

1½ ounces rum
1 ounce cream of coconut

2 ounces pineapple juice
½ cup crushed ice

Blend at low speed for 10 to 15 seconds. Pour over ice cubes in a tall glass. Garnish with a pineapple chunk and cherry on a toothpick.

GREEN LIZARD FROM WILSON

One 6 ounce can frozen limeade
6 ounces Vodka

10 fresh mint leaves
Ice cubes to fill blender

Place first three ingredients in blender. Fill blender with ice cubes. Frappe. Garnish glasses with sprig of fresh mint.

"Pig eyed!"

MAMA'S MIMOSAS

1 quart orange juice

1 bottle chilled champagne

This is a light tasty pickup for any special breakfast or brunch. The yield is 10 to 12 servings.

GELATINE PUNCH

Two 3 ounce packages
  strawberry or cherry gelatine
4 cups boiling water
1½ cups cold water
One 8 ounce can frozen
  concentrated lemon juice

One 48 ounce can pineapple
  juice
1 quart ginger ale

Dissolve gelatine in boiling water until completely dissolved. Add cold water, one can of concentrated lemon juice at room temperature and one 48 ounce can pineapple juice. Do not refrigerate this. Add cold ginger ale just before serving. Serves 25 guests.

FRUIT PUNCH FOR A CROWD

24 ounces orange juice
24 ounces grapefruit juice
24 ounces pineapple juice
30 ounces lemon-lime soft drink

30 ounces grape juice
30 ounces apple juice
One 16 ounce can fruit cocktail
30 ounces of ginger ale

Combine and chill. A portion of this punch can be frozen in a gelatin ring. Float the ring in the center of the punch bowl to keep it chilled. Great for a before or after games party. This serves 25 guests.

L.C.'S MILK PUNCH

6 ounces half and half
2 teaspoons powdered sugar
2½ ounces bourbon

Dash of vanilla
Nutmeg to garnish

Combine all ingredients in shaker and mix well. Pour over cracked ice. Top with nutmeg. The yield is 2 servings.

"Through the lips, over the gums, look out tummy here it comes!"

CHRISTMAS WASSAIL PUNCH

1 gallon apple cider
Two 46 ounce cans pineapple
  juice
One 8 ounce can concentrated
  lemon juice

One 16 ounce can frozen
  orange juice
8 cinnamon sticks
2 heaping tablespoons whole
  cloves

Mix juices and simmer on low heat. Wrap spices in a cheesecloth bag, and drop into liquid. Simmer for 20 to 30 minutes. Serves 20.

POP'S SODA POP SLUSH

1 quart gingerale
2 quarts strawberry, grape, or
   orange soda
One 6 ounce package of
   gelatine (same flavor as soda)

2 packages unsweetened
   flavored drink mix
1 cup sugar

Make gelatine according to package directions. Make unsweetened drink mix according to directions but do not add sugar. Mix all other ingredients and then stir in sugar until dissolved. Put in large plastic container with lid and freeze in freezer overnight. Take out and stir. Freeze two more hours then stir again. Can add other liquid such as pineapple juice to keep it slushy. Kids love this on a hot summer day.

RED HOT RAZORBACK TEA

1 gallon tea
Juice from 8 oranges
Juice from 6 lemons

1 ounce red hots
One 10 ounce bottle ginger ale
Sugar to taste

Mix juices, tea, red hots and sugar. Heat until "piping hot". Add ginger ale just before serving.

HOLIDAY SPICED TEA

2 cups sugar
3 cups water
2 sticks cinnamon
1 teaspoon whole cloves
1 tablespoon crystalized ginger

2 family sized tea bags and 7
   cups water
1½ cups mixed orange juice
   (fresh or canned)
6 tablespoons lemon juice

Bring to boil sugar, 3 cups of water, cinnamon, cloves, and crystalized ginger. Mix and leave overnight. Next make stong tea with the 7 cups water and two family sized tea bags. Take out spices and add orange juice and lemon juice. Mix with other ingredients and refrigerate. Will keep one week. Serve warm or hot. The yield is approximately 15 cups.

YELLVILLE YELLOW BIRD

2 cups orange juice
2 cups pineapple juice
1½ cups light rum
1 cup Galliano
¼ cup cream de banana

Ice
Garnishes of orange slices,
    maraschino cherries, and
    pineapple cubes

Combine liquids and mix well. Pour over ice-filled tall glasses. Garnish. This summer treat can be frapped. It is guaranteed to make you wake up with yellow feathers in your mouth! The yield is 6 to 8 servings.

"Dizzingly good!"

Breads

CATHEAD BISCUIT MIX

8 cups all-purpose flour
2 teaspoons salt
⅓ cup baking powder

4 to 5 teaspoons sugar
(optional)
1 cup shortening

Mix all dry ingredients together and cut in shortening until mixture resembles coarse meal. A food processor is great to use for mixing the ingredients. Store mixture in the refrigerator to keep fresh. Use as you would any biscuit mix. When making biscuits use ½ cup buttermilk for each cup of mix. Make pancakes or waffles as you would with any pancake mix.

"Makin' Cathead Biscuit Mix!"

DAYBREAK BISCUITS

5 cups all-purpose flour
1½ teaspoons salt
½ teaspoon soda
1 cup buttermilk, lukewarm

2 packages yeast
5 tablespoons warm water
3 tablespoons sugar

Mix all dry ingredients together except yeast and set aside. Dissolve yeast in the warm water. Cut in shortening into dry ingredients by using a fork or best done in a food processor. The mixture will look like meal. Mix buttermilk with warm water and yeast. Then add to flour mixture. Roll out dough onto floured board and cut with biscuit cutter ½ to 1 inch thick. Place biscuits on ungreased cookie sheets and let rise slightly. Bake in 400 degree oven for 12 to 15 minutes.

RAISIN BISCUIT WEDGES

3 cups all-purpose flour
3 teaspoons baking powder
2 tablespoons sugar
½ teaspoon baking soda
1 teaspoon salt

½ cup solid vegetable
  shortening
1 cup buttermilk
¼ cup dark seedless raisins
1 egg white, slightly beaten

Blend together flour, baking powder, sugar, salt, and soda in a bowl. Cut shortening into flour mixture until it resembles coarse meal. Add buttermilk and raisins and stir until well blended. Divide dough into 3 parts. On a floured board roll each part into a circle about ⅓ inch thick. Cut each into 5 wedges and place on an ungreased baking sheet. Brush tops with egg white. Bake in 425 degree oven for 12 to 15 minutes. Great served warm with butter and your favorite jam or jelly.

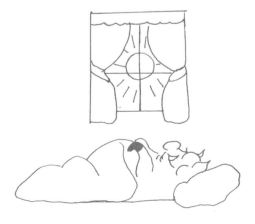

PUMPKIN PATCH BREAD

4 eggs
3 cups sugar
1 cup vegetable oil
⅔ cup water
2 cups canned pumpkin
3½ cups all-purpose flour

2 teaspoons soda
1½ teaspoons salt
1 teaspoon cinnamon
1 teaspoon nutmeg
May use ½ to 1 cup raisins

Blend eggs, sugar, and oil in large mixing bowl. Add water and canned pumpkin, mixing well. Mix all dry ingredients together, then gradually add to other mixture, until well blended. Bake in two greased and floured loaf pans at 350 degrees for one hour. May bake in small coffee cans that have been greased and floured. This is great for gifts at Christmas time. Use raisins in bread if desired.

HOT CROSS BUNS

4¼ to 4½ cups all-purpose flour
⅓ cup sugar
1 teaspoon salt
2 packages active dry yeast
¾ teaspoon ground cinnamon
¾ cup milk

½ cup water
½ cup margarine
2 eggs
½ cup currants
1 egg yolk, beaten
2 tablespoons cold water

FROSTING:
½ cup powdered sugar

1½ tablespoons milk

Combine 1 cup flour, sugar, salt, cinnamon and yeast. Heat milk, water and margarine until very warm (120 degrees to 130 degrees). Add to dry ingredients and beat 2 minutes at medium speed. Add ½ cup flour and 2 eggs. Beat at high speed 2 minutes. Add more flour to make a very stiff dough. Stir in currants. Cover tightly. Refrigerate at least 2 hours. May leave up to a day.

Turn out onto floured board, and shape into 18-20 round balls. Arrange in 2 well greased 8 inch square cake pans. Combine egg yolk and 2 tablespoons water and brush buns. Cover and let rise until doubled around 1 hour.

Cut a cross on the top of each bun with a sharp knife. Bake at 375 degrees 20 to 25 minutes. Cool. Frost with powdered sugar frosting.

HOME TOWN CORNBREAD

1 cup yellow cornmeal
1 cup all-purpose flour
2 tablespoons sugar, optional
4 teaspoons baking powder

½ teaspoon salt
1 cup milk
1 egg
¼ cup vegetable oil

Combine cornmeal, flour, sugar, baking powder, and salt. Mix throughly. Add milk, egg and vegetable oil. Beat until smooth, about one minute. Bake in greased 8 inch square baking pan or 8 inch skillet in preheated hot oven (400 degrees to 425 degrees) 15 to 20 minutes.

"Bein' Hoggish!"

FATTENING FRENCH DOUGHNUTS

⅓ cup sugar
½ cup warm water
2 tablespoons vegetable oil
½ teaspoon salt
½ cup evaporated milk

1 package or cake yeast
¼ cup warm (not hot) water
4 cups sifted all-purpose flour
2 eggs, beaten

In a large mixing bowl combine sugar, warm water, oil, salt, and evaporated milk. Mix yeast with warm water until dissolved. Add yeast and water to other liquids and mix throughly. Beat eggs and add to mixture. Stir in flour. Make sure mixture is well blended. If necessary add a little more flour to make the dough soft and not sticky. Turn dough out on a lightly floured board and knead lightly for 5 or 6 minutes. Knead dough until smooth and elastic. Place dough in an oiled bowl and cover with a damp cloth. Let dough rise in a warm place for ½ hour, the dough should double in size. Punch down dough and turn out on a lightly floured board. Divide dough into 3 portions, roll out one portion, while covering the other two. Roll the dough into a rectangle ½ inch thick. Cut into triangles or rectangles about 1½ inch to 1 inch. Punch center in on each doughnut so it will be thinner in the center. Fill a heavy skillet or fry pan ⅓ full of oil and heat. You will have to test the oil for frying, too low a heat will cause dough to soak up too much oil and the center will not get done if the oil is too hot. Fry and brown on each side evenly. Drain on paper towels. When cool, shake in plastic bag of powdered sugar.

These will also freeze well. Cool after frying and freeze in tightly closed container. If going to freeze do not use the confectioners sugar. Heat in oven as you take out of freezer and dust with sugar while warm. The yield is 4 to 5 dozen.

SOUTHERN SWEETDOUGH CINNAMON LOAF

Southern sweet dough
1 cup sugar

2 teaspoons cinnamon
Melted butter

Roll sweet dough about ½ inch thick and brush both sides with melted butter. Combine sugar and cinnamon. Sprinkle this over dough and roll up in jelly-roll fashion. Let rise in greased loaf pan. Bake at 350 degrees for 30 minutes.

BLUEBERRY OATMEAL MUFFINS

3 cups biscuit mix
½ cup packed brown sugar
¼ cup quick cook oatmeal
1 teaspoon cinnamon

2 eggs, well beaten
1½ cups milk
2 cups fresh blueberries
2 tablespoons butter

Combine biscuit mix, sugar, oatmeal and cinnamon. Mix eggs, milk and butter. Stir in dry ingredients to egg mixture. Stir until blended. Fold in blueberries. Spoon into greased muffin pans and bake in preheated oven at 400 degrees for 15-18 minutes. The yield is 18 muffins.

PEANUT BUTTER CORN FLAKE MUFFINS

1 cup milk
1¾ cups corn flakes
½ cup peanut butter
½ cup firmly packed brown
 sugar

1 egg
2 tablespoons vegetable oil
1¼ cups all-purpose flour
1 tablespoon baking powder
½ teaspoon salt

Preheat oven to 400 degrees. Mix together cereal and milk in a large bowl; let stand a few minutes to soften cereal. Add peanut butter, egg, sugar, and oil. Beat until well blended. Combine flour, baking powder and salt; mix well. Add to cereal mixture, mixing only slightly. Fill 12 greased medium sized muffin cups ¾ full. Bake at 400 degrees for 15 to 20 minutes. The yield is 1 dozen.

HOME TOWN PEANUT BUTTER MUFFINS

½ cup peanut butter
1¼ to 1½ cups flour
1 cup milk
2 eggs

¾ cup vegetable shortening
2 heaping teaspoons baking
 powder
¼ teaspoon salt

Melt shortening, when cooling add peanut butter. Mix well. Mix dry ingredients together and blend well. Add milk and eggs to peanut butter mixture. Stir in all dry ingredients and beat until well blended. Bake in 350 degree oven for 20 to 25 minutes.

BLUEBERRY BEAR PANCAKES

One 13 ounce box blueberry
   muffin mix with canned
   blueberries
⅓ cup flour

1 egg, beaten
1 cup milk
1 tablespoon vegetable oil

Drain blueberries, rinse and set aside. Mix remaining ingredients and gently fold in blueberries. Cook "bear" shaped pancakes on hot griddle. Serve with butter and syrup.

BUTTON POPPIN POPOVERS

6 egg whites
4 tablespoons vegetable
   cooking oil

2 cups milk
2 cups sifted all-purpose flour
½ teaspoon salt

Beat egg whites with oil and milk.

Mix the flour and salt in a large bowl; and add liquids gradually, beat with an electric mixer until well blended. Mix for 2 minutes.

Oil 12 large or 18 medium muffin cups and fill each ½ full of batter. Place in cold oven. Turn oven to 350 degrees and bake 45 to 60 minutes, or until popovers are brown. Serve with your favorite jams or jellies. The yield is 12 large or 18 medium popovers.

15 MINUTE DINNER ROLLS

2 cups of your homemade
   biscuit mix or prepackaged
   mix

½ can cold beer
1 tablespoon sugar

Mix all ingredients together and spoon into 12 greased muffin tins. Bake for 15 minutes.

QUICK HOUR AND A HALF DINNER ROLLS

2 to 2½ cups unsifted
  all-purpose flour
2 tablespoons sugar
½ teaspoon salt

1 package dry yeast
½ cup milk
¼ cup water
2 tablespoons margarine

Mix ¾ cup flour, sugar, salt and undissolved yeast. Heat milk, water and margarine to 120-130 degrees. Gradually add to dry ingredients and beat 2 minutes at medium speed of mixer. Add ¼ cup flour. Beat at high speed 2 minutes. Stir in enough additional flour to make soft dough. On floured board knead 2 to 3 minutes. Divide dough into 12 equal pieces. Shape into balls. Place in greased 8 inch round pan. Pour a 1 inch depth of boiling water into large pan on bottom rack of cold oven. Set rolls on rack above water. Cover. Close oven door: let rise 30 minutes. Uncover rolls: Remove pan of water. Turn oven to 375 degrees. Bake 20-25 minutes or until done. Remove from pan to cool. Serve warm. Makes 1 dozen rolls.

SOUTHERN SWEETDOUGH CINNAMON ROLLS

¾ cup sugar
1 teaspoon cinnamon

⅓ cup raisins (optional)
Southern sweet dough

FROSTING:
½ cup powdered sugar

1½ tablespoons milk

Roll dough ½ inch thick. Combine sugar, cinnamon and raisins. Sprinkle over dough. Roll up in jelly-roll style, seal edges and slice into 1½ inch thick rolls. Place in greased pans. Cover and let rise one hour. Bake at 350 degrees for 20 to 25 minutes. Frost or serve plain. The yield is 18 to 24 rolls.

SUNDAY MORNIN' CINNAMON ROLLS

2 packages yeast
2 cups warm water
½ cup sugar
2 teaspoons salt

6 tablespoons shortening,
  melted
4½ to 5½ cups flour

FILLING:
½ cup margarine
1 cup sugar

1 tablespoon cinnamon
(optional - chopped nuts)

ICING:
½ box powdered sugar

¼ cup milk

Mix yeast and water, stir until yeast is dissolved. Add rest of ingredients and mix well with wooden spoon or in food processor. Shape dough in a ball in center of bowl. Cover and let rise until double, about 1 hour. Pat out on floured board. Roll into a 12 x 24 inch rectangle. Melt the stick of margarine and spread evenly on dough. Sprinkle sugar and cinnamon mixture over margarine. Add chopped nuts if desired. Roll dough jellyroll fashion and seal edges. Cut in 1 inch wedges. Put on greased cookie sheets or in cake pans. Cover and let rise 1 hour or cover with foil and refrigerate overnight, then let rise 2 hours. Bake 20-25 minutes at 375 degrees. Ice while hot. The yield is 2 dozen rolls.

SOUTHERN SWEET DOUGH

1 cup all-purpose flour
¼ cup sugar
1 package dry yeast
1 teaspoon salt
⅝ cup milk

⅛ cup butter
1 egg
1½ cups additional all-purpose
  flour

Heat butter and milk over low heat until liquid is warm. Combine gradually with 1 cup flour, sugar, yeast and salt. Add egg and mix well. Beat in remaining flour. Knead until smooth on floured board for about 10 minutes. Place in a greased bowl, grease top, cover, and place in a warm place. Let rise for about 1 hour or until it doubles in size.

Punch dough and let rest another 10 minutes. Shape into coffeecakes, rolls, loafs, or pinwheels.

FANCY FRENCH TOAST

8 slices white bread or thinly
   sliced french bread
4 eggs, beaten
4 tablespoons milk
2 tablespoons sugar

Dash of salt
Dash of nutmeg or cinnamon
   (optional)
Powdered sugar for dusting

Combine all ingredients except bread. Dip bread into mixture, coating both sides. Fry slowly in butter until browned on both sides. Dust with powdered sugar. Serve with maple syrup, grape jelly or whatever strikes your fancy. The yield is 4 servings.

SIMPLE FRENCH TOAST

4 eggs, beaten
2 tablespoons sugar
6 slices white or wheat bread

2 tablespoons butter
Powdered sugar

Beat eggs with sugar. Heat skillet or grill with butter. Pour eggs into shallow bowl or pan. Dip each piece of toast into egg mixture turning quickly. Coat both sides of bread but don't let the bread soak up too much of the egg mixture. Fry until lightly browned. Sprinkle with powdered sugar or serve with jelly or syrup.

"Got a case of the hungries for Spoon Bread!"

APPLETON SPOON BREAD

APPLE MIXTURE:

4 cups coarsley chopped
   cooking apples
¼ cup cornstarch
¼ cup brown sugar

1 teaspoon cinnamon
¼ teaspoon nutmeg
2 cups apple juice

PUDDING MIXTURE:
2 cups milk
½ cup cornmeal
3 tablespoons margarine
1 tablespoon sugar

½ teaspoon cinnamon
⅛ teaspoon nutmeg
3 eggs, beaten

Arrange apples in a greased baking dish. Combine apple mixture ingredients and cook over a medium heat until thickened. Pour over apples. Combine pudding mixture. Cook over low heat, stirring constantly, until thickened. Pour over apples and apple mixture. Bake for 45-50 minutes at 350 degrees. The yield is 6 servings.

SPRINGDALE SPOON BREAD

1 cup cornmeal
1 cup water
2 cups milk

1 teaspoon salt
3 eggs, well beaten
¼ cup melted margarine

Scald water and milk. Add cornmeal and salt. Cook until thickened. Add beaten eggs and margarine. Stir and pour into greased casserole. Bake at 350 degrees for 1 hour. The yield is 4 to 6 servings.

Cakes
and
Frostings

HEAVENLY ANGEL FOOD CAKE AND FLUFFY PINEAPPLE FROSTING

One large angel food cake
One 3½ ounce package instant
  vanilla pudding
One 15 to 16 ounce can
  pineapple

One 16 ounce carton non dairy
  whipped topping

Slice angel food cake to make two layers. Mix together pineapple with juice and the instant pudding. Fold this into topping and ice between layers of cake. Finish icing rest of cake. This makes a pretty fluffy icing. Might use fresh strawberries and juice rather than pineapple for a different flavor.

"Hoggie Heaven"

ANGEL FOOD SURPRISE LOAF

1 cup milk
1 cup sugar
3 egg yolks
3 egg whites
1 envelope unflavored gelatine

1 teaspoon vanilla
1 teaspoon almond extract
½ pint whipping cream
1 angel food cake

ICING:
½ pint whipping cream,
  whipped and sweetened

One 14 ounce package coconut

Cook milk, sugar and egg yolks in double boiler until thick, then add envelope of gelatine. Stir until gelatin is dissolved. Cook 2 minutes. Cool mixture. When cool add vanilla, and almond extract. Fold in stiffly beaten egg whites and whipping cream, stiffly whipped. Rub off the crumbs on a small angel food cake and break cake into bite size pieces. Pour custard mixture over angel food pieces and mix throughly. Pour into two oiled loaf pans. Put in refrigerator for eight hours or longer. This also freezes well for later use. Ice with sweetened whipping cream and coconut.

TEX-ARK-ANA BANANA SPLIT CAKE

CRUST:
2 cups graham cracker crumbs   ½ cup butter
2 tablespoons sugar

FILLING:
1 cup butter   One 9½ ounce carton non dairy
2 eggs   topping
2 cups powdered sugar   ¼ cup chopped pecans
4 bananas   ⅛ cup chopped cherries
1 large can crushed
   pineapple/drained

Combine crust ingredients and pat into 13 x 9 inch pan. Bake at 350 degrees for 20 minutes. Beat butter, eggs and powdered sugar until smooth and fluffy. Pour over crust. Slice 4 bananas over mixture. Drain crushed pineapple and spoon over bananas. Spread carton of non dairy topping over pineapple. Sprinkle with chopped pecans and cherries. Refrigerate, do not freeze! The yield is 6 to 8 servings.

FIRST PRIZE CARROT CAKE

2½ cups sifted cake flour   2¼ cups sugar (may substitute
2 teaspoons baking powder   brown sugar for half)
2 teaspoons cinnamon   2 teaspoons salt
4 eggs   1½ cups vegetable oil
3 cups grated carrots

ICING:
3 ounce packages cream   1 pound powdered sugar
   cheese (softened)   2 teaspoons vanilla
¼ cup butter   ¾ cup pecans

Mix all dry ingredients together and then set aside. Cream sugar and oil together and add eggs. When well blended add dry ingredients then grated carrots. Bake in 350 degree oven for 30 to 40 minutes. Be sure to prepare your baking pans with plently of shortening and flour. You may use 3 eight or nine inch pans or one large rectangle cake pan for baking.

ICING: Soften cream cheese and butter by letting it warm out of the refrigerator for one hour. Cream together cream cheese and butter then add powdered sugar and vanilla. When will blended add pecans. Cool cake before icing.

DAIRY DELIGHT CHEESE CAKE

18 ounces cream cheese
1 pint sour cream
2 eggs

1 cup sugar
One 9 inch graham cracker
   crust

Mix softened cheese, sour cream, eggs and sugar together until well blended. Pour into a graham cracker crust and bake at 350 degrees for 30 to 40 minutes.

MYRENE'S NO BAKE CHEESE CAKE

2 envelopes unflavored gelatin
1 cup sugar (divided)
¼ teaspoon salt
2 eggs separated
1 cup milk

1 cup heavy cream whipped
1 teaspoon grated lemon rind
3 cups cottage cheese
1 tablespoon lemon juice
1 teaspoon vanilla

CRUMB TOPPING: (Can be doubled if desired)
2 tablespoons melted butter
1 tablespoon sugar
½ cup graham cracker crumbs

¼ teaspoon cinnamon
½ teaspoon nutmeg

Mix together gelatin, ¾ cup sugar, and salt in top of double broiler. Beat together egg yolks and milk and mix with gelatin mixture. Cook over boiling water stirring constantly (about 10 min.) until thick. Remove from heat, add lemon rind and then cool. Stir in cottage cheese, lemon juice, and vanilla. Chill, stirring occasionally until mixture molds slightly when dropped from a spoon. Beat egg whites until stiff (not dry). Gradually add ¼ cup sugar until very stiff. Fold into gelatin and cheese mixture. Fold in whipped cream. Turn into pan with half of Crumb Topping on bottom. Sprinkle other half of topping on top of cheese cake.

CRUMB TOPPING: Mix ingredients and line pan in wax paper and sprinkle crumb topping in botom of pan (save half for top).

43

BIG FLAT CHOCOLATE COLA CAKE

2 cups unsifted flour
2 cups sugar
1 cup butter
3 tablespoons cocoa
1 cup cola

½ cup buttermilk
2 beaten eggs
1 teaspoon soda
1 teaspoon vanilla
1½ cups miniature
    marshmallows

ICING:
½ cup butter
3 tablespoons cocoa
6 tablespoons cola

1 box powdered sugar
1 cup chopped pecans toasted

Combine flour and sugar in bowl. Heat butter, cocoa and cola to boiling and pour over flour sugar mixture, mixing thoroughly. Add buttermilk, eggs, soda, vanilla and marshmallows after mixing together. Mix well. This will be a thin batter with marshmallows floating on the top. Bake in prepared pan, 1 inch deep big flat cookie sheet. Bake in 350 degree oven for 30 to 35 minutes. Ice while hot.

Icing: Combine butter, cocoa and cola and heat to boiling. Pour over powdered sugar. After beating well, add 1 cup chopped pecans which were toasted while oven was preheating. Spread over hot cake.

BIG FORK BUTTERMILK CHOCOLATE CAKE

2 cups sugar
½ cup shortening or margarine
2 eggs
1 teaspoon soda
3 tablespoons cocoa

1 teaspoon vanilla
2 cups all-purpose flour
½ cup buttermilk
1 cup boiling water

FROSTING:
4 tablespoons cocoa
6 tablespoons milk
½ cup margarine or butter

1 box powdered sugar
1 teaspoon vanilla

Cream together sugar and shortening. Add eggs, soda, cocoa and vanilla. Blend well. Mix in flour, alternating buttermilk, and boiling water. Bake in greased and floured rectangle pan or 9 inch cake pans. Bake 20-25 minutes at 375 degrees. When cake is cool bring to boil the ingredients cocoa, milk, and butter. Remove from heat. Add one box of powdered sugar and 1 teaspoon of vanilla. When well blended ice cake.

MOUNTAIN HOME CHOCOLATE CINNAMON CAKE

2 cups all-purpose flour
2 cups sugar
½ cup butter or margarine
4 tablespoons cocoa
½ cup vegetable oil
1 cup water

2 eggs
½ cup buttermilk
1 teaspoon soda
1 teaspoon cinnamon
1 teaspoon vanilla

FROSTING:

Bring to boil:	½ cup butter or margarine
	4 tablespoons cocoa
	6 tablespoons milk
Remove from heat and add:	1 teaspoon vanilla
	1 box confectioners' sugar
Beat until smooth and add:	1 cup chopped pecans

Sift or mix together flour and sugar. Bring to boil 1 stick of butter or margarine, cocoa, ½ cup oil and 1 cup water. Remove from heat and add to first mixture. Mix well. Add eggs, buttermilk, soda, cinnamon and vanilla. After blended well pour into greased 11 x 16 deep cookie sheet or large cake pan. Bake 25 minutes at 375 degrees. Five minutes before cake is done fix frosting. Ice as soon as cake comes from oven.

CHOIR CAKE

1¾ cups all-purpose flour
½ teaspoon salt
6 egg whites
6 egg yolks
1½ cups sugar

6 tablespoons fresh squeezed
 orange juice
1 tablespoon grated orange
 peel
Powdered sugar

Beat egg whites until stiff peaks form gradually adding ¾ cup of sugar. Beat egg yolks until very thick, about 3 minutes, gradually adding ¾ cup of sugar. Sift flour with salt. Add flour mixture and orange juice alternately into egg yolk mixture. Gently fold into beatened whites. Add orange peel. Pour into bundt or tube pan and bake in a preheated oven, 350 degrees, 40-55 minutes, or until cake springs back when pressed with finger. Cool, loosen from pan, shake to release and place on serving plate. Dust with powdered sugar. The yield is 12 servings.

TOADIE'S FAVORITE FIG CAKE

2 cups all-purpose flour
1 teaspoon cinnamon
1 teaspoon cloves
1 teaspoon nutmeg
1 teaspoon salt
1 teaspoon soda
1 teaspoon vanilla

1 cup vegetable oil
1½ cups sugar
1 cup buttermilk
3 eggs
1 cup fig preserves (with juice and chopped)
1 cup chopped pecans

SAUCE:
1 cup sugar
½ cup buttermilk
1 teaspoon vanilla

1 tablespoon white corn syrup
½ teaspoon salt
¼ to ½ cup butter

Mix all dry ingredients then add oil and beat well. Add eggs one at a time, alternating with the milk. Add figs and vanilla. Bake in greased and floured tube pan at 350 degrees for one hour. When cake is done mix sauce. Mix all ingredients in saucepan and boil three minutes stirring constantly. Pour over hot cake. Let cake cool in pan.

"Yore eyes are bigger than yore tummy!"

GRANDMOTHER DUKE'S WHITE FRUITCAKE

1 cup butter
1 cup sugar
5 eggs, beaten
4 cups pecans
One 4 ounce container of
    glazed cherries
One 4 ounce container of
    glazed pineapple

1 pound mixed fruit
½ pound raisins
1¾ cups all-purpose flour
½ teaspoon baking powder
½ ounce lemon extract
½ ounce vanilla
½ cup dates chopped (optional)

Cream together sugar and butter until fluffy, add beaten eggs and cream again. Then combine all the ingredients. Bake at 300 degrees until slightly rising then lower to 250 degrees for 2 hours or until done. A greased and floured bundt pan is great for baking this cake.

NO BAKE FRUIT CAKE

1 pound candied cherries
1 pound candied pineapple
1 pound raisins
3 cups pecans
1 pound graham crackers,
    crushed

1 pound marshmallows
One 12 ounce can evaporated
    milk

Melt marshmallows in evaporated milk over low heat. Add graham crackers and fruit. This will be stiff batter. Mix well and then pour into loaf pans or an angel food cake pan greased with margarine. Refrigerate over night. For an extra touch you could decorate top with cherries and pineapple. You can use any mixture of candied fruit in the cake as long as you use 2 pounds of candied fruit.

HALLELUJAH CAKE

2 tablespoons butter or
   margarine
One 8 ounce package cream
   cheese
2¼ cups sugar
1 tablespoon corn starch
3 eggs
2 tablespoons plus 1⅓ cups
   milk
1½ teaspoons vanilla extract

2 cups all-purpose flour
1 teaspoon baking powder
½ teaspoon soda
½ cup butter
Four 1 ounce squares
   unsweetened chocolate
   (melted)
1 teaspoon salt

FROSTING:
¼ cup milk
¼ cup butter
One 6 ounce package
   semi-sweet chocolate chips

1 teaspoon vanilla extract
2½ cups confectioners sugar

Cream 2 tablespoons butter with cheese, ¼ cup sugar and corn starch. Add 1 egg, 2 tablespoons or milk, and ½ teaspoon vanilla extract. Beat at high speed until creamy. Grease and flour a 13 x 9 inch cake pan. Combine flour with 2 cups sugar, salt, baking powder, and soda in a large bowl. Add ½ cup butter and 1 cup milk and blend at low speed. Add remaining ⅓ cup milk, 2 eggs, and chocolate. Add vanilla extract and blend well. Spread ½ of batter in pan. Spoon cheese mixture over all chocolate batter. Top with remaining chocolate batter and bake at 350 degrees for 50 to 60 minutes. Makes you want to shout HALLELUJAH!

Frosting: combine milk and butter in saucepan and bring to a boil. Remove from the heat and blend in chocolate chips. When melted, stir in vanilla and confectioners' sugar. Beat until ready to spread.

OZARK MOUNTAIN JAM CAKE

3 cups all-purpose flour
1 cup sugar
1 cup butter
1 cup buttermilk
1 tablespoon soda
6 egg yolks
6 egg whites

1 tablespoon cinnamon
1 tablespoon allspice
1 cup chopped pecans
1 cup fig preserves
1 cup blackberry jam
1 cup strawberry preserves

Cream butter and sugar together until smooth. Add jam and preserves. Beat egg yolks; add yolks to creamed preserve mixture and blend well. Combine flour and spices. Add soda to buttermilk. Add buttermilk and flour alternately to creamed mixture. Stir in pecans.

Fold stiffly beaten egg whites into batter.

Bake in 3 well-greased cake pans for 50 minutes at 350 degrees. Cool before frosting. Use Ozark Mountain Frosting.

"Let's use a measure of elbow grease."

49

MAXINE'S HUMMINGBIRD CAKE

3 cups all-purpose flour
2 cups sugar
1 teaspoon cinnamon
1 teaspoon soda
1 teaspoon salt
1½ cups vegetable oil

3 eggs
1 teaspoon vanilla
One 8 ounce can crushed
  pineapple, including juice
2 cups diced bananas

Mix well, preferably with a spoon. Bake for 1 hour and 20 minutes at 350 degrees in a greased and floured pan.

BODCAW BROWN SUGAR POUND CAKE

1 cup butter
½ cup shortening
1 pound light brown sugar
1 cup sugar
5 eggs
3 cups all-purpose flour

½ teaspoon salt
1 teaspoon baking powder
1 cup milk
1 teaspoon vanilla
Powdered sugar to sprinkle on
  cake

Beat butter and shortening together: gradually add the sugar, creaming until mixture is light and fluffy. Beat in eggs one at a time. Sift together dry ingredients and add alternately with milk and vanilla to the creamed mixture. Pour batter into greased and floured 10 inch tube pan. Bake at 350 degrees for 1 hour and 15 minutes, or until done when tested with a straw or toothpick. Cook 10 minutes, then remove from pan. Dust with powdered sugar by sprinkling a little on top of cake.

GREG'S FUDGE CENTER POUND CAKE

1½ cups butter or margarine
6 eggs
1½ cups sugar
2 cups all-purpose flour

1 package chocolate fudge
  frosting mix, best double
  fudge
2 cups walnuts (optional)

Cream butter in large bowl or food processor at high speed. Add eggs and sugar. Continue creaming at high speed until light and fluffy. Add flour and frosting mix, blending well. Add walnuts if desired. Pour batter into greased bundt pan. Bake at 350 degrees for 60 to 65 minutes. Cool 2 hours: remove from pan. Cool completely before serving.

PRIZE WINNING PRUNE CAKE

2 cups sugar
1 cup vegetable oil
3 eggs
1 tablespoon soda
1 cup buttermilk
1 cup prunes (cooked, seeded, and mashed)

1 cup nuts
2 cups all-purpose flour
1 teaspoon allspice
1 teaspoon salt
2 teaspoons nutmeg
2 teaspoons cinnamon

Cream together sugar and oil. Beat in eggs one at a time. Dissolve soda in 1 cup buttermilk. Add buttermilk, prunes, and nuts to sugar and oil mixture. After sifting together dry ingredients, mix into other mixture. Pour into greased and floured bundt pan. Bake 1 hour and 20 minutes in 350 degree oven.

MOUNT IDA'S COCONUT - LEMON PUDDING CAKE

2 eggs separated
¼ teaspoon cream of tartar
¼ cup lemon juice
1 teaspoon grated lemon peel
1 cup milk
1 cup sugar

¼ cup all-purpose flour
¼ teaspoon salt
¼ cup toasted coconut
Whipped topping
Maraschino cherries

Beat egg whites and cream of tartar in large mixing bowl until stiff peaks form and set aside. Beat egg yolks slightly. Beat in lemon peel, lemon juice, and milk. Add sugar, flour and salt. Beat until smooth. Fold this mixture into beaten egg whites. Pour into 1 quart casserole.

Pour 1 cup of very hot water into a 1½ quart casserole in oven. Set casserole of pudding mixture in casserole of water. Bake at 350 degrees for 20 to 25 minutes or until wooden toothpick inserted in center comes out clean. Sprinkle with toasted coconut. Serve with whipped topping and a cherry on top. The yield is 6 servings.

CAKES AND FROSTINGS

DOWN HOME SHORTCAKE

½ cup soft butter or margarine
½ cup sugar
1 egg
¼ teaspoon salt

2 teaspoons baking powder
1 cup all-purpose flour
½ cup milk

Mix all ingredients together and pour into a greased 8 x 12 inch pan. Lightly sprinkle with a tablespoon of sugar. If you use a glass pan, bake at 450 degrees for 15 to 20 minutes. If you use a metal pan bake at 375 degrees for 30 minutes. Serve with fresh strawberries in sugar or fresh peaches in sugar. Top with whipped cream.

SOUR CREAM COCONUT CAKE

1 box white cake mix
¾ cup vegetable oil
3 eggs
One 8 ounce carton of sour
  cream

One 8 ounce can cream of
  coconut

Mix all ingredients. Bake at 350 degrees for 30 to 40 minutes in greased and floured 8 or 9 inch cake pans.

STRAWBERRY PATCH CAKE

½ cup vegetable oil
4 eggs (separate yolks and
  whites)
2 teaspoons vanilla
1 cup sugar
2 cups flour

½ teaspoon salt
3 teaspoons baking powder
½ box strawberries
One 3 ounce package
  strawberry gelatine
¼ cup milk

FROSTING:
½ cup butter or margarine
1½ pounds powdered sugar
½ box strawberries (frozen that
  are thawed)

1 teaspoon vanilla

Cream together yolks, sugar, and oil. Add milk and vanilla and blend well. Mix together all dry ingredients and add to liquid mixture. Blend well. Beat egg whites until stiff and fold into cake mixture. Bake in two 8 or 9 inch cake pans that are greased and floured. Bake at 350 degrees for 30 minutes or until cake springs back when touched. When cake is cool, mix frosting. Cream together butter, powdered sugar, strawberries and vanilla. You may want to use less powdered sugar if you use less juice with the strawberries.

CANEHILL SUGAR CANE CAKE

1¼ cups boiling water
1 cup oats
½ cup butter (softened)
1 cup granulated sugar
1 cup firm brown sugar
1¼ teaspoons vanilla

2 eggs
1½ cups sifted all-purpose flour
1 teaspoon soda
½ teaspoon salt
¾ teaspoon cinnamon
¼ teaspoon nutmeg

FROSTING:
¼ cup butter or margarine
   melted
½ cup firmly packed brown
   sugar

3 tablespoons half and half
⅓ cup chopped nutmeats
¾ cup shredded or flaked
   coconut

Pour boiling water over oats, cover and let stand 20 minutes. Beat butter until creamy; gradually add white and brown sugar. Beat until fluffy. Blend in vanilla and eggs. Stir in oats. Sift together flour, soda, salt, and spices. Add to creamed mixture and mix well. Pour into well greased and floured 9 inch pan. Bake at 350 degrees for 55 minutes.

When cake is done mix frosting. Cream together butter with sugar. Add half and half and blend well. Add chopped nuts and coconut. Spread on cake and broil under broiler until it bubbles.

VICEY'S VANILLA WAFER CAKE

1 cup margarine or butter
2 cups sugar
6 eggs slightly beaten
1 cup chopped pecans
1 can angel flake coconut

1 - small box vanilla wafers
   crushed by rolling pin or food
   processor
½ cup sweet milk

Crush vanilla wafers then add other ingredients. Dough will be stiff (not as runny as regular cake dough). Bake in 300 degree oven for 1½ hours. (Baking it slow and long is the secret of the cake.)

WHITEHALL WHITE CAKE
With Chocolate Curls

1 white cake mix
Two 1 ounce squares
  unsweetened chocolate,
  coarsely shaved

Mix cake mix according to directions on package. Fold into mix coarsely shaved chocolate. Bake in 2 layer, 8 or 9 inch pans that are greased and floured. Bake according to package directions. Prepare the Dark Chocolate Filling and put this between layers of cake when cake is cool. Frost with our Best Ever Seven Minute Frosting, spreading over sides and top of cake. Sprinkle with shaved chocolate to decorate.

WHITEHALL WHITE CAKE
Chocolate Filling

1 cup sugar
⅓ cup light cream
Two 1 ounce squares
  unsweetened chocolate,
  broken into pieces

2 egg yolks, beaten
2 tablespoons butter or
  margarine

In medium saucepan, mix sugar, cream, butter, and chocolate. Cook over medium heat, stirring constantly, until chocolate and butter are melted.

Stir about half of mixture into egg yolks. Put this back into remaining mixture in saucepan. Heat to boiling, stirring constantly. Boil and stir 1 minute. Remove from heat and cool completely.

BERTHA'S BROWN SUGAR ICING

1 cup brown sugar
1 cup white sugar
1 cup evaporated milk

½ cup butter
¼ cup all-purpose flour
2 teaspoons vanilla

Melt butter and add flour. Cook until thick then add sugar and milk. Cook until sugar is dissolved. Add 2 teaspoons vanilla. Cool until icing thickens. Great icing on a spice cake. Sprinkle cake with ¼ cup chopped maraschino cherries, ½ cup raisins, ½ cup chopped pecans. Great! This recipe will ice a two layer cake or a sheet cake.

OZARK CARAMEL FROSTING

3¼ cups sugar   1⅔ cups milk
1 cup butter

Caramelize sugar and butter in heavy iron skillet over high heat. Stir constantly! Add milk slowly, still stirring; cook until warm and smooth. Beat frosting until it holds its shape. Use this frosting with Ozark Mountain Jam Cake.

GLORIA'S TWO MINUTE CHOCOLATE ICING

1 cup butter   ½ cup milk
½ cup cocoa   1 teaspoon vanilla
2 cups sugar

Combine ingredients in saucepan. Let mixture come to a rolling boil. Cook two minutes. Be sure to time this as longer cooking makes it sugary. This will seem thin. But let it cool and stir until it begins to thicken. Use to cover brownies, cake or cupcakes. Don't forget to lick the spoon when you're finished!

JENNIFER'S LEMON CREAM ICING

2 cups sugar   2 teaspoons lemon peel
⅔ cup evaporated milk   1 teaspoon lemon juice
½ cup butter

Mix sugar, evaporated milk, and butter in a large saucepan. Boil for 8 minutes, stirring occasionally. Remove from heat and add lemon peel and lemon juice. Beat and then ice cake immediately. Great on a prepackaged lemon or yellow cake mix.

BEST EVER SEVEN MINUTE FROSTING

One 7 ounce jar marshmallow
  cream
3 egg whites
1 cup sugar

3 tablespoons water
½ teaspoons cream of tartar
½ teaspoon vanilla

Combine all ingredients except vanilla. Cook in double boiler 2 to 7 minutes. Beat while cooking with electric mixer. Add vanilla when frosting stands in peaks. Frosting will frost a two layer cake or a sheet cake.

FOOD GROUPS

Fat: each portion contains 45 calories
1 Teaspoon   -   butter, oil, mayonnaise
1 Tablespoon -   dressings, cream

Bread: each portion contains 68 calories
1 slice   -   bread
1   biscuit, muffin, roll, cornbread (2 inch piece)
½ cup   cereal, rice, grits, spaghetti, dried beans, and peas

Milk: each portion contains 170 calories
1 cup   -   whole, skim, buttermilk
½ cup   -   evaporated
¼ cup   -   powdered dry

Fruits: each portion contains 40 calories
1 small   -   apple, figs, orange, pear, banana, peach
¼ cup   -   grape juice
½ cup   -   applesauce, grapefruit juice, orange juice, pineapple
1 cup   -   watermelon, strawberries, blackberries, raspberries
2 medium   -   plums, prunes, apricots
1 large   -   tangerine

Vegetables: may be eaten in reasonable amounts as desired.
                   Calorie amounts are negligible.

Meats: each portion contains 73 calories
1 ounce   -   meat, poultry, fish, cheese
1   egg, hot dog
¼ cup   tuna, crab, lobster, salmon, cottage cheese
2 teaspoons   peanut butter
1 slice   -   luncheon meat

(See chart on page 128)

Candies
and
Cookies

FLAUDIE'S PEANUT BRITTLE

2 cups sugar
½ cup water
1 tablespoon butter
1 teaspoon vanilla

1 cup corn syrup
2½ cups raw peanuts
1 teaspoon salt
2 teaspoons soda

Cook sugar, syrup, and water until mixture spins a thread, then add raw peanuts. Cook until golden brown. Add butter, vanilla, salt, and soda. Mix and pour out on two large cookie sheets that have been buttered. Let candy cool and break into pieces. Store in tight covered container.

FRESH CRACKED PECAN BRITTLE

1 cup margarine
1 cup sugar

2 tablespoons light corn syrup
2 cups pecans

Using a coated skillet, combine margarine, sugar, and syrup, stirring constantly, bring to a boil and boil 12 to 14 minutes. (No longer). It will be pulling away from the sides and light brown in color. Add pecans and spread in a thin layer on greased foil which has been spread with margarine. Let harden and break into pieces.

SATURDAY NIGHT DATE NUT BALLS

½ cup butter
¾ cup sugar
**One 8 ounce package chopped
  dates**

2½ cups crispy rice cereal
1 cup finely chopped pecans
Can flaked coconut

Combine butter, sugar, and dates in saucepan. Bring to a boil and stir constantly for about 3 minutes. Stir in rice cereal and pecans and cool to touch. With butter on your hands shape into 1 inch balls. Roll in coconut. The yield is 4 dozen candies.

"Shake, Rock and Roll!"

CANDIES

LIP SMACKIN' PEANUT BUTTER FUDGE

2 cups sugar
⅔ cup milk
2 tablespoons light corn syrup

1 teaspoon vanilla
¼ cup butter
1 cup peanut butter

Combine sugar, milk, and syrup in large saucepan and cook over medium heat until mixture begins to boil. Stir constantly to avoid scorching. Cook approximately 2 to 3 minutes or until mixture forms soft ball when dropped in cold water. Take off heat and add vanilla, butter, and peanut butter. Beat by hand until mixture begins to thicken. Pour into small square cake pan that is well buttered.

SOUTHERN ORANGE BALLS

One 12 ounce package vanilla
  wafers (crushed)
1 pound box powdered sugar
½ cup margarine, softened
One 6 ounce can frozen orange
  juice thawed and undiluted

1 cup finely chopped nuts
One 7 ounce can flaked
  coconut (to be used to cover
  outside of orange balls)

Crush vanilla wafers then add other four ingredients after they have been mixed together; powdered sugar, margarine, frozen orange juice, and chopped nuts. Form into small balls about one inch or 1½ inches then roll in coconut. Freeze and serve frozen. The yield is approximately 6 dozen.

GEORGEANNA'S ENGLISH TOFFEE

2 cups melted butter (1 pound)
2 cups sugar
¼ cup water
2 tablespoons light corn syrup

½ to ¾ cup slivered almonds
8 to 10 ounces sweetened
  chocolate bars (broken into
  pieces) For topping

Mix all ingredients together and boil to soft crack stage using candy thermometer. Keep stirring until candy reaches the hard crack stage. At this time add the ½ to ¾ cup of slivered almonds. Turn out candy onto a buttered cookie sheet. While still hot quickly break up 8 to 10 ounces of sweetened chocolate. When melted smooth over chocolate on top of candy with a knife.

WASHINGTON'S FAVORITE CANDY

FILLING:

1 cup butter	1 can condensed milk
2 pounds powdered sugar	2 teaspoons vanilla
4 cups chopped pecans	

COATING:

1 large package chocolate chips   ¼ pound paraffin

Mix ingredients for filling. Chill. Roll into small balls, place on waxed paper and chill again. Melt chocolate chips and paraffin. Dip chilled balls into chocolate mixture. Place on waxed paper.

I JUST LOVE THOSE BROWNIES

2 cups sugar	½ cup cocoa
1 cup butter	2 cups pecans
4 eggs	1 teaspoon vanilla
1½ cups all-purpose flour	½ teaspoon salt

Cream butter and sugar until smooth. Add eggs one at a time, blending well after each. Add dry ingredients. Stir in pecans last. Bake in preheated oven at 350 degrees for 25 minutes. Cover with two minute chocolate icing for a sinfully delicious tasty lip smacking treat!

"I just love those brownies!"

BUDDY BEAR'S BUTTER COOKIES

1 pound butter
1 pound box light brown sugar
1 egg, beaten
6 cups flour

1 teaspoon vanilla
1 cup chopped pecans
(optional)

Mix ingredients. Roll in waxed paper and refrigerate. Slice and bake at 300 degrees for 6 to 8 minutes. Watch baking time closely to prevent burning!

GRANDMA'S TEA CAKES

3⅔ cups all-purpose flour
2½ teaspoons baking powder
½ teaspoon salt
⅔ cup shortening
1½ cups sugar
2 eggs

1 teaspoon vanilla or almond
extract
4 teaspoons milk (add more if
needed)
Candy cookie decorations

Cream together sugar and shortening. Add eggs, milk, and flavoring. Mix together all dry ingredients, then add to liquid. Roll dough on floured board to ¼ inch thickness. Cut with favorite cookie cutters dipped in flour. Place on greased cookie sheet, sprinkle with cookie decorations, and bake at 350 degrees until lightly browned.

ELLA MAY'S ITALIAN COOKIES

½ cup butter
1 cup sugar
4 eggs (keep one egg yolk out)
2 tablespoons Bourbon whiskey

3 teaspoons baking powder
3 cups all-purpose flour
1 cup chopped pecans

Preheat oven to 350 degrees. Cream butter and sugar together. Add eggs and blend. Mix together flour and baking powder then mix to other mixture. Add pecans. Grease cookie sheet well. Shape dough into two or three 2 inch wide loaves. Brush tops with beaten egg yolk. Then cook 20 minutes until top is slightly browned. Cut loaves into ½ to 1 inch slices. After slices are cut toast them lightly on each side. These freeze very well.

MCCLARTY'S MACAROONS

⅓ cup flour
2¼ cups shredded coconut
⅛ teaspoon salt

⅔ cup sweetened condensed
   milk
1 teaspoon vanilla

Preheat oven to 250 degrees. Mix flour, salt and coconut. Add condensed milk and vanilla. Drop cookie dough by large spoonfuls onto greased cookie sheet. Bake for 20 minutes or until brown. The yield is 2 dozen cookies.

MOLASSES CRINKLES

¾ cup shortening
1 cup brown sugar
1 egg
¼ cup molasses
2¼ cups all-purpose flour

2 teaspoons soda
¼ teaspoon salt
½ teaspoon cloves
1 teaspoon cinnamon
1 teaspoon ginger

Cream together ¾ cup shortening, brown sugar, egg, and molasses. Mix together flour, soda, salt, cloves, cinnamon, and ginger. Add dry ingredients to other mixture. Blend well. Chill dough. Roll into balls the size of large walnuts. Dip tips in sugar. Place sugared side up 3 inches apart on greased cookie sheet. Sprinkle each cookie with 2 or 3 drops of water to produce a cracked surface. Bake until set, but not hard, in a 375 degree oven for 10 to 12 minutes. The yield will be 4 dozen 2½ inch cookies. This dough also makes great cut out gingerbread cookies, by rolling the dough out on a floured surface to about an ⅛ inch thickness and cutting with your favorite gingerbread cookie cutter.

"Long sweetenin'"

65

"How sweet it is!"

OLD FASHIONED MOLASSES OATMEAL COOKIES

1¼ cups sifted all-purpose flour
¾ teaspoon baking soda
½ teaspoon salt
½ teaspoon baking powder
½ cup shortening (solid)
½ cup sugar

½ cup molasses
2 eggs
1½ cups quick oats, uncooked
1 cup raisins, optional
1 cup chopped nuts, optional

Sift flour, baking soda, salt, baking powder into mixing bowl. Add remaining ingredients and mix until well blended. Drop by heaping teaspoons two inches apart onto an ungreased cookie sheet. Bake for 10 to 12 minutes in a 350 degree oven. The yield is about 4 dozen cookies.

OAKHILL NO BAKE OATMEAL COOKIES

2 cups sugar
3 tablespoons cocoa
½ cup butter or margarine
½ cup milk

Salt
3 cups oatmeal
½ cup peanut butter
1 teaspoon vanilla

Mix in medium saucepan sugar, cocoa, butter, milk, and salt. Bring to boil and cook one minute. Take off heat and add oatmeal, peanut butter, and vanilla. Mix well and drop by teaspoons onto waxed paper to cool.

You can substitute 2½ cups oats and ½ cup of coconut for a different taste.

CRISPY BUTTERSCOTCH OATMEAL COOKIES

One 6 ounce package
  butterscotch chips
¾ cup butter
2 tablespoons boiling water
1 teaspoon baking soda

2 cups oats (uncooked)
1 cup sifted all-purpose flour
¾ cup sugar
Dash salt

Preheat oven to 350 degrees. Combine chips and butter and melt in double boiler. Remove from heat when melted. Mix boiling water with baking soda and add to butterscotch mixture. Gradually blend into other ingredients. Drop by spoonfuls on an ungreased cookie sheet. Bake 10 minutes at 350 degrees. The yield is 5 dozen cookies.

PICNIC PEANUT BUTTER COOKIES

½ cup butter
½ cup crunchy or smooth
  peanut butter
½ cup brown sugar
½ cup granulated sugar
1 egg

1¾ cups all-purpose flour
Dash of salt
1 teaspoon vanilla
1 teaspoon soda
1 package candy kisses
  (unwrapped)

Cream butter with peanut butter. Add sugar and blend well. Add egg. Mix together flour, salt, and soda. Add to other mixture. When well blended add vanilla. Roll dough into balls about the size of a walnut, then roll in sugar. Cook on cookie sheet at 350 degrees until light brown and cracked looking (about 7 minutes). Put candy kisses in center, flattening out the dough to cookie shape (cookies will crack some more). Cook for 3 or 4 more minutes.

POLLYANNA COOKIES

1 cup graham cracker crumbs
¼ cup butter
1 can flaked coconut
One 6 ounce package chocolate
  chips

One 6 ounce package
  butterscotch chips
1 can sweetened condensed
  milk
1 can chopped pecans

Melt butter and combine with graham cracker crumbs. Pat down mixture into bottom of 9 x 12 inch baking pan. Layer each ingredient. Bake at 325 degrees for 30 minutes. Cut when cooled.

CHARLOTTE'S LEMONADE SUGAR COOKIES

1 cup butter or margarine
2 eggs
1 cup sugar
3 cups all-purpose flour
1 teaspoon soda

One 6 ounce can frozen
lemonade concentrate,
thawed
Sugar

Cream together butter and one cup of sugar. Add eggs and beat until fluffy. Add soda, mix well. Add lemonade concentrate. Blend well. Add flour. When well blended, drop dough by a teaspoon. Bake two inches apart on ungreased cookie sheet. Bake in 400 degree oven for 7 to 9 minutes or until lightly browned. While hot brush cookies lightly with water and sprinkle with sugar. The yield is 4 dozen small cookies.

TIMOTHY'S THUMBPRINT COOKIES

¼ cup soft butter
¼ cup shortening
¼ cup brown sugar
1 egg separated

1 teaspoon vanilla
1 cup all-purpose flour
¼ teaspoon salt
¾ cup chopped nuts

Cream together butter, shortening, and brown sugar. Add egg yolk, vanilla and blend well. Sprinkle in salt and then add flour, mixing well. Dip one teaspoon of dough, rolled in a ball into the egg white that has been beaten with a fork. Roll ball of dough in chopped pecans. Place on greased cookie sheets and press in center with thumb. Bake at 350 degrees until brown. Fill each cookie with your favorite jelly.

Fish
and
Seafood

DEGRAY BASS DELIGHT

1 - 3 pounds fillet of bass
½ cup butter
2 teaspoons lemon juice
1 tablespoon chablis or
 vermouth

⅛ teaspoon pepper
½ cup Parmesan cheese
Seasoned salt
Paprika

Preheat oven to 475 degrees. Rub fillets with salt and pepper. Place in oven, flesh side up in butter. Bake until lightly brown. Turn and bake an additional 15 minutes. Turn again and baste with drippings. Sprinkle each piece with lemon juice, wine, cheese and paprika. Bake 5 to 7 minutes. Broil under broiler for 2 minutes. Baste with drippings and watch carefully!

CRAB NEWBURG

¼ cup butter
½ teaspoon salt
2 tablespoons all-purpose flour
⅛ teaspoon cayenne
2 cups light cream
3 slightly beaten egg yolks

6 ounces of fresh or frozen
 crab, thawed if frozen
1½ tablespoons dry sherry
Cooked rice
⅛ teaspoon nutmeg

Melt butter over low heat in a medium saucepan. Mix together flour, salt, nutmeg and cayenne. Add to butter and stir until smooth. Gradually add cream. Cook over medium heat 8 to 10 minutes or until slightly thickened, stirring constantly. Gradually add ¾ cup hot sauce mixture to egg yolks, beating to blend. Add egg yolk mixture to remaining sauce mixture. Blend well. Add crab and liquid. Cook 2 to 3 minutes or until thickened, stirring constantly. Remove from heat. Stir in sherry. Serve over hot, cooked rice. Decorate with parsley or other vegetables. The yield is 4 to 6 servings.

"Better than a Collard Sandwich!"

HOT CRAB SANDWICH CASSEROLE AU PULASKI

8 slices bread
Butter or margarine
One 7 ounce package of king
  crab

½ pound sharp cheese
4 eggs
3 cups milk

Cut crust from 8 slices of bread. Butter bread and place 4 slices in a 3 x 8 inch baking dish. Drain crab and break apart. Place crabmeat over bread. Shred cheese and sprinkle over crab. Top with remaining slices of bread. Mix 4 eggs and 3 cups of milk. Pour egg mixture over bread. Let casserole soak several hours. Bring to room temperature then bake at 325 degrees or until golden brown.

SPRING RIVER SALMON CROQUETTES

One 15½ ounce can red or pink
  salmon
10 crushed soda crackers
¾ cup all-purpose flour
½ teaspoon baking powder

2 eggs (slightly beaten)
⅛ teaspoon black pepper
1 tablespoon grated onion or
  onion flakes (optional)

Take salmon from the can and remove bones. Flake salmon in bowl. Mix ¼ cup of flour with baking powder, and pepper. Add eggs, crushed crackers, and onion. Mix thoroughly. Make five or six balls rolling each in remaining ½ cup of flour. When each croquette is covered well with flour fry in small skillet filled half full of hot cooking oil. Fry until golden brown.

DEEP SOUTH DEEP SEA CASSEROLE

1 pound fish, cut in bite size
   pieces
¼ pound scallops, cut into
   small pieces

¼ pound crabmeat
¼ pound small shrimp
One 10¾ ounce can Cheddar
   cheese soup

Mix all ingredients together and pour into a greased casserole dish. Bake 30 minutes at 400 degrees. Serve with white or wild rice.

"Goin' Fishin'"

MILLWOOD BROILED FISH FILLETS

2 pounds fish fillets or steaks
1 teaspoon salt
Dash pepper
¼ cup margarine or butter

1 tablespoon lemon juice
½ teaspoon parsley flakes,
   optional

Cut fish into serving size portions. Baste both sides with lemon juice and melted margarine. Sprinkle both sides with salt and pepper and place on greased broiler pan about 2 to 3 inches from broiler, skin side up. Broil 6 to 8 minutes or until slightly browned. Baste with margarine and lemon juice and turn carefully. Brush top side with lemon juice and butter and broil another 6 to 8 minutes or until fish flakes easily with a fork. The yield is 4 servings.

SAMANTHA'S BAKED FLOUNDER

2 pounds flounder fillets or
  steaks
1 teaspoon seasoned salt
1 cup milk

1 cup cracker crumbs
¼ teaspoon paprika
¼ cup margarine

Make sure fillets or steaks are cut into serving size portions. Add seasoned salt to milk. Dip fish in milk and roll in cracker crumbs, mixed with paprika. Place fish in a greased baking pan. Dot each piece with margarine. Bake in hot oven at 500 degrees for 10 to 15 minutes or until fish flakes with a fork. The yield is 4 servings.

FLOUNDER AND VEGETABLE DINNER

2 pounds flounder fillets (8 to
  10 fillets)
1 tablespoon all-purpose flour
1 large size (14 inches x 20
  inches) oven cooking bag
Seasoned salt
1 cup (4 ounces) shredded
  Cheddar cheese or Colby
  cheese
2 medium zucchini, cut in ½
  inch diagonal slices
1 medium tomato, chopped,
  seeds removed

1 cup sliced fresh mushrooms
¼ cup chopped green onion
1 teaspoon basil leaves
¼ teaspoon pepper
⅛ teaspoon garlic powder
2 tablespoons butter or
  margarine, diced
Paprika
2 small yellow squash, cut in ½
  inch round slices

Preheat oven to 350 degrees. Shake flour in oven cooking bag. Place bag in 13 x 9 x 2 inch baking pan. Sprinkle fish with seasoned salt and cheese. Roll each fillet starting at narrow end. Place fish rolls seam side down in center of bag, forming two rows. Combine vegetables, basil, pepper and garlic powder. Arrange vegetables in bag around fish rolls.

Sprinkle fish with paprika; dot with butter. Close bag with nylon tie; make 8 half-inch slits in top. Bake 20 to 25 minutes or until fish flakes easily with fork. The yield is 4 to 5 servings.

JUMPIN' FRIED FROG LEGS

8 frog legs
1 tablespoon milk
1 egg
1 teaspoon salt

½ teaspoon pepper
½ cup all-purpose flour
½ cup cornmeal

Wash and dry legs. Combine egg and milk. Mix together salt, pepper, flour, and cornmeal. Dip frog legs into egg mixture and then roll in flour-meal mixture. Let dry for 1 hour. Fry in deep hot oil, heated to 375 degrees. Fry until golden brown, approximately 3 to 5 minutes or until tender.

BROILED LOBSTER TAILS "DEQUEEN"

6 to 9 ounces lobster tail per person

Butter
Paprika

Split each lobster tail the entire length of shell exposing meat. Broil shell side up, 5 to 6 inches from heat, under broiler, for 5 to 6 minutes. Turn and repeat process. Baste with butter frequently to reserve moisture in lobster meat. Garnish with paprika. Serve with melted butter, now fit for de Queen!

HOLLARING BOILED LIVE LOBSTERS

Place enough water into a large pot to cover lobsters. Add 1 tablespoon of salt. When water begins to boil, drop in the live lobsters. Begin timing when water returns to boil.

1 to 1½ pounds	10 - 12 minutes
1½ to 2 pounds	12 - 15 minutes
2½ to 5 pounds	20 - 30 minutes
6 to 10 pounds	35 - 50 minutes

The lobster will be done when the shell turns bright red.

OUT OF THE ORDINARY SEAFOOD CASSEROLE

¼ pound crabmeat

1 pound fish, cut into small
  pieces

¼ pound scallops, cut into
  small pieces

¼ pound small shrimp

One 10¾ ounce can Cheddar
  cheese soup

Mix all ingredients together and pour into greased casserole dish. Bake at 400 degrees for 30 minutes. Great served over wild or white rice. The yield is 4 servings.

ALMA'S RED SNAPPER

1½ pounds red snapper fillets
½ teaspoon salt
½ cup margarine or butter
2 tablespoons chopped parsley
⅛ teaspoon garlic salt
1 tablespoon lemon juice
¼ teaspoon grated lemon rind

½ teaspoon dried crushed
  thyme leaves
⅓ cup toasted slivered almonds
Paprika
Any cooked vegetable to
  decorated dish

Place fish in 12 x 8 x 2 inch dish. Sprinkle with salt and garlic salt. Dot with 2 tablespoons of margarine or butter. Cover with aluminum foil and bake at 375 degrees for 10 minutes. Uncover and baste with pan drippings and bake another 20 minutes. Melt remaining butter and add all other ingredients except paprika and almonds. Warm mixture. Before serving stir in almonds. Remove fish to warm serving platter and sprinkle with paprika. Decorate with your favorite vegetable. Pour sauce over fish. The yield is 4 servings.

SEAFOOD IMPERIAL

Three 6 ounce cans crabmeat
8 slices of bread, diced
1½ pounds cooked shrimp
½ cup mayonnaise
1 small onion, chopped
1 bell pepper, chopped

1 cup chopped celery
4 eggs
3 cups milk
One 10 ounce can cream of
  mushroom soup

Place half of the bread in a greased baking dish. Mix crabmeat, shrimp, onion, pepper, celery, and mayonnaise. Spread mixture over bread. Cover with remaining bread. Mix eggs and milk. Pour over bread. Bake at 350 degrees for 15 minutes. Remove from oven, pour soup over mixture and top with cheese. Continue to bake for 1 hour.

BARBECUED LITTLE ROCK SHRIMP

5 pounds shrimp (raw, deheaded, and in the shell)
1 package instant Italian Dressing (mix according to package but use red wine vinegar)

1 cup butter
2 ounces pepper (black)
Juice from two lemons

Combine all ingredients and bake at 375 degrees for one hour in a covered dish. Shrimp fans will come from miles around to sample this one.

LAFAYETTE SHRIMP CREOLE

1½ pounds raw shrimp (peeled and cleaned)
½ cup butter
½ green pepper, chopped fine
½ onion, chopped fine
½ stalk celery, chopped fine
½ teaspoon parsley flakes
One 8 ounce can tomato sauce
One 6 ounce can tomato paste

½ teaspoon thyme
½ teaspoon oregano
½ teaspoon cayenne or red pepper
½ teaspoon cumin
¼ teaspoon black pepper
⅛ teaspoon salt
⅛ teaspoon garlic salt

Sauté onions, celery, and green peppers in butter. Add all seasonings. Add all other ingredients, except shrimp. Cook slowly over low heat for 20 minutes. Add shrimp and cook another 30 minutes. If sauce is too thick thin with a ¼ of a cup of water. Serve over rice.

QUICK SHRIMP GUMBO

½ cup vegetable oil
2 cups sliced fresh okra
1 pound fresh or frozen shrimp, peeled and deveined
⅔ cup chopped green onions and tops
3 cloves finely chopped garlic

1½ teaspoons salt
½ teaspoon pepper
2¼ cups water
One 14 ounce can tomatoes
7 drops hot pepper sauce
2 bay leaves
2 or 3 cups cooked rice

Sauté okra in oil 10 minutes. Add onions, shrimp, garlic, salt, and pepper. Cook about 5 to 8 minutes. Add tomatoes, water, and bay leaves. Cover and simmer 25 minutes. Add pepper sauce. Be sure to remove bay leaves before serving. Serve over cooked rice. The yield is 6 servings.

STUTTGART RICE AND SHRIMP CANTONESE

3 cups hot cooked rice
12 ounces peeled, deveined raw
   shrimp, halved lengthwise
3 tablespoons butter, margarine
   or oil
2 cups sliced onions
2 cups diagonally sliced celery
1 quart (8 ounces) fresh
   spinach leaves

One 14 ounce can fancy mixed
   Chinese vegetables
¼ teaspoon pepper
¼ cup soy sauce
1¼ cups chicken broth
2 tablespoons cornstarch

Cook rice. Saute shrimp in butter for 1 minute or until shrimp turns pink, using a large skillet. Add celery and onions. Cook for 2 minutes, while stirring. Add spinach and Chinese vegetables which have been rinsed and drained. Cover and cook 1 minute. Mix together pepper, soy sauce, chicken broth, and cornstarch. Stir into shrimp-vegetable mixture. Cook, stirring, until sauce is clear and thickened about 2 minutes. Serve over rice.

PAN FRIED "DOVER" SOLE

1 pound fresh dover sole
Butter

Flour

Dredge sole in flour. Melt butter. When pan is hot, fry sole in butter until lightly browned on each side and flakey. This is easy and delicious. The yield is 2 servings.

FISH AND SEAFOOD

BATESVILLE WHITE RIVER TROUT AMANDINE

2 pounds gulf trout fillets or
   other fresh fillets
¼ cup all-purpose flour
1 teaspoon seasoned salt
1 teaspoon paprika
¼ cup melted butter or
   margarine

½ to ¾ cup sliced almonds
2 tablespoons lemon juice
4 to 5 drops liquid hot pepper
   sauce
1 tablespoon chopped parsley

Cut fillets into 5 or 6 portions. Combine flour, seasoned salt, and paprika. Roll portions in flour mixture and place in a single layer, skin side down. In a well greased baking dish pour 2 tablespoons melted butter over portions. Broil about 4 inches from source of heat for 10 to 15 minutes or until fish flakes easily when touched with a fork. While broiling fish, saute almonds in remaining butter until golden brown, stirring constantly. Remove from heat and mix in lemon juice, hot pepper sauce, and parsley. Pour over fish and serve at once. The yield is 4 to 6 servings.

NORFORK LAKE TROUT

2 pounds skinless trout fillets
2½ tablespoons onion, grated
⅛ teaspoon pepper
1½ teaspoons salt
2 large tomatoes, chopped into
   small pieces

¼ cup melted butter or
   margarine
1 cup Swiss cheese, shredded

Place fillets in a single layer on a well greased baking dish. Sprinkle with onion, salt, and pepper. Cover with chopped tomato. Pour melted butter over fillets and broil about 4 inches from the heat for 10-12 minutes, or until fish flakes easily when tested with a fork. Sprinkle fish with cheese and broil 2 to 3 minutes longer, or until cheese melts. The yield is 4 to 6 servings.

Fowl
and
Poultry

CHICKEN A LA CREMA

4 chicken breasts, split into
  halves
1 cup sliced mushrooms
½ cup butter

½ cup burgundy wine
½ cup orange juice
1 cup heavy cream
Salt and pepper to taste

Sauté chicken and mushrooms in butter; add wine, cook slowly until liquid is reduced to ½ original amount. Add orange juice and cream. Season to taste. Continue to cook until the liquid is reduced to a glaze. The yield is 4 servings.

ALMA'S CHICKEN BREASTS IN WINE

3 tablespoons butter
8 boneless, skinless chicken
  breast halves
One 4 ounce can sliced
  mushrooms, drained

½ cup white wine
¼ teaspoon tarragon

Brown chicken breasts in butter. Add wine, mushrooms, and tarragon. Continue to cook, covered, until tender. The yield is 6 servings.

AUNT BUSBY'S SWEET AND SOUR CHICKEN FINGERS

4 boneless, skinless chicken
  breasts, cut into strips
2 tablespoons vegetable oil
One ⅞ ounce package sweet
  and sour sauce mix
One 8 ounce can pineapple
  chunks (drain and reserve
  juice)

1 tablespoon brown sugar
1 green bell pepper, cut into
  strips
¼ cup water

Brown chicken in hot oil. Combine water, sauce mix, sugar, and pineapple juice and pour over chicken. Add bell pepper and pineapple chunks. Cover and cook over low heat for 15 to 20 minutes. The yield is 4 servings.

BARTHOLOMEW LEMON BAKED CHICKEN

¼ cup soy sauce or teriyaki
  sauce
¼ cup lemon juice

Paprika
4 chicken breasts

Wash and skin chicken breast. Mix together lemon juice and soy or teriyaki sauce. Let chicken soak in mixture for one or two hours. Place chicken breast right side up on greased baking dish and pour a small amount of sauce over each breast. Sprinkle lightly with paprika. Bake uncovered at 350 degrees for one hour or until golden brown. If you would like to bake a whole chicken, cut it in serving pices and mix equal amounts of lemon juice and soy or teriyaki sauce.

BEEBE'S LEMON-MARINADE CHICKEN BARBECUE

4 chicken halves
1 cup vegetable oil
½ cup lemon juice
1 tablespoon salt
1 teaspoon paprika

2 teaspoons basil
2 teaspoons onion powder
½ teaspoon thyme
1 crushed garlic clove

Place chicken halves or quarters in shallow baking dish. Combine all ingredients and pour over chicken. Cover and marinate in refrigerator for 6 hours or overnight, turning chicken often. Place chicken on grill, brushing often with marinade. Grill on each side at least 25 minutes. Chicken may also be cooked in the oven or under the broiler. The yield is 6 to 8 servings.

"Sunday goin' to meetin' Barbecue!"

CHICKEN IN MAGNOLIA MUSHROOM SAUCE

Six ½ chicken breasts
One 10¾ ounce can cream of
  mushroom soup
One 8 ounce carton sour cream
One 4 ounce can sliced
  mushrooms

¼ cup cooking sherry (optional)
Salt and pepper
Paprika

In glass baking dish, place breasts skin side up. Sprinkle lightly with salt and pepper. In bowl, mix soup, sour cream, mushrooms and juice, and cooking sherry. Pour over breasts. Sprinkle with paprika. Bake at 350 degrees for one hour or until done. Serve over rice.

CREAM CHEESE CHICKEN DARDANELLE

6 chicken breasts, without
  bones
Pepper
6 slices bacon
1 package dried beef

Two 10 ounce cans of cream of
  chicken soup
One 8 ounce package cream
  cheese
1½ cups sour cream

Pepper chicken breasts, wrap each in bacon and place on layer of dried beef in bottom of casserole dish. Mix remaining ingredients and pour over chicken breasts. Cover with foil. Bake for 2 hours at 325 degrees. Remove foil and allow chicken breasts to brown lightly. Serve over rice. The yield is 4 to 6 servings.

EVENING SHADE CHICKEN IN WINE SAUCE

¾ cup wine (any kind)
¼ cup soy sauce
¼ cup vegetable cooking oil
2 tablespoons water
1 clove garlic
1 teaspoon ginger

1 teaspoon oregano
1 tablespoon brown sugar
One 2½ ounce can or jar sliced
  mushrooms and juice
6 chicken breasts (skin
  removed)

Mix all ingredients together. Marinate chicken for several hours in mixture. Leave in the liquid mixture. Cover and bake for 1½ to 2 hours at 350 degrees. Serve over rice. Pour off mixture and use as a gravy on the rice if so desired.

"Plum tuckered out!"

HOME SWEET HOME CHICKEN BREASTS

8 chicken breasts halves
One 8 ounce bottle Russian
  dressing

One 6 ounce jar apricot
  preserves
1 package dried onion soup mix

Mix well and pour over chicken breasts. Bake covered at 325 degrees for 1 hour or until tender. The yield is 4 to 6 servings.

LITTLE FLOCK CHICKEN SUPREME

One 2½ ounce jar dried beef
5 whole chicken breasts or 10
　halves (Boned and skinned)
10 strips of bacon
One 10¾ ounce can cream of
　mushroom soup

One 4 ounce can mushroom
　stems and pieces (drained)
One 8 ounce carton sour cream
Salt and pepper

Grease glass baking dish and line bottom of dish with dried beef chips. Take chicken breasts that have been boned and skinned and wrap in bacon strips. Secure bacon with toothpicks. Salt and pepper chicken to taste. Mix can of cream of mushroom soup with can of mushrooms, and carton of sour cream. Dilute sauce with mushroom juice if needed. Pour this mixture over chicken and bake at 350 degrees for 1½ to 2 hours. Cover with foil to keep chicken from drying out.

LITTLE ITALY CHICKEN CACCIATORE

1 medium size onion (chopped)
1 green pepper (diced)
3 tablespoons margarine, olive
　oil, or vegetable oil
1 broiler-fryer cut in serving
　size pieces
1 teaspoon salt
⅛ teaspoon pepper

1 clove garlic minced
One 14 ounce can tomatoes
One 3 ounce can whole
　mushrooms
1 tablespoon wine vinegar
½ teaspoon rosemary
½ teaspoon sugar

Sauté onion and green pepper in one tablespoon of salad oil for five minutes. Remove from skillet and set aside. Sprinkle chicken with salt and pepper. Brown until golden brown in remaining 2 tablespoons of oil and add garlic. Return onion and green pepper to pan. Add tomatoes, chicken, mushrooms, vinegar, rosemary, and sugar. Cover lightly and simmer 45 minutes or until chicken is tender when pierced with a fork.

NASHVILLE BAKED CHICKEN WITH PEACHES

1 cut up broiler-fryer chicken,
  or 2½ pounds of chicken
  parts
1 tablespoon all-purpose flour
1 teaspoon monosodium
  glutamate, flavor enhancer,
  (optional)

½ teaspoon salt
1 tablespoon butter
One 1 pound can peach halves
½ teaspoon each cinnamon,
  and nutmeg

Place chicken in a shallow baking dish. Combine flour, glutamate and salt: sprinkle over chicken pieces. Dot with butter. Bake uncovered in a moderate oven at 375 degrees for 30 minutes. Drain syrup from the peaches: Reserve ½ cup, place peach halves around chicken. Spoon reserved syrup over chicken and peaches. Sprinkle with cinnamon and nutmeg. Bake 20 minutes longer. The yield is 6 servings.

PIKE COUNTY SWEET AND SOUR BAKED CHICKEN

½ cup chopped onion
¼ cup butter or margarine
½ cup coarsely chopped green
  pepper
½ cup coarsely chopped
  carrots
¾ cup ketchup
1 cup pineapple juice
2 tablespoons vinegar
¼ cup firmly packed brown
  sugar

1 tablespoon soy sauce
½ teaspoon garlic salt
½ teaspoon salt
¼ teaspoon pepper
Dash ground red pepper
Dash ground ginger
1 cup pineapple chunks,
  drained
One 3 pound broiler-fryer
  chicken, cut up

Preheat oven to 400 degrees. In medium skillet, heat butter until melted, add onion, green pepper and carrots and cook 5 minutes, stirring. Stir in ketchup, pineapple juice, vinegar, sugar, soy sauce, garlic salt, salt, pepper and ginger. Cook stirring constantly, until mixture boils. Add pineapple chunks. Arrange chicken pieces skin side up in greased 13 x 9 x 2 inch baking dish. Pour sweet and sour sauce over all. Bake covered 45 minutes. Uncover and bake about 30 minutes longer, or until chicken is done.

PRAIRIE GROVE SMOTHERED CHICKEN

4 large chicken breast halves
½ cup sherry
One 4 ounce can button mushrooms

One 8 ounce carton sour cream
One 10 ounce can cream of mushroom soup

Combine ingredients. Pour over chicken breasts in uncovered baking dish. Bake at 350 degrees for 1 to 1½ hours. The yield is 2 to 4 servings.

"Fallin' in for vittles!"

QUEEN WILHELMINA CHICKEN LOAF

1 hen boiled, boned, and chopped
2 cups soft bread crumbs
2 cups cooked rice
One 2 ounce can pimentoes
1 cup milk

3 eggs
⅛ teaspoon onion salt
⅛ teaspoon celery salt
Salt and pepper to taste
2 cups chicken broth
One 2½ ounce can mushrooms

Sauce: 1 cup mushroom soup thinned with broth. Add chopped giblets.
Mix all ingredients and let stand in buttered loaf pan for 1 hour or 1½ hours. Cook until brown at 350 degrees. Serve sauce over loaf.

SMOTHERED CHICKEN WITH MUSHROOM GRAVY

1 large fryer
One 10¾ ounce can cream of
  mushroom soup
¼ cup butter or margarine

Salt and pepper
One can of water (use soup can
  to measure)

Melt butter or margarine in large skillet which has a lid. Cut up fryer in serving pieces if not already cup up. Salt and pepper chicken. Fry until meat turns a golden brown. Chicken may not be done. Add one can of cream of mushroom soup after mixing soup well with one can of water. Simmer over low heat for 30 to 40 minutes. Serve over rice, creamed potatoes, or egg noodles.

SPRINGDALE CHICKEN WITH VEGETABLES

1 whole chicken cut into pieces
2 tablespoons butter
1 onion, cut into wedges

1 tomato, cut into wedges
1 zucchini, cut into pieces
Salt and pepper to taste

Brown chicken in butter in large skillet. Add vegetables. Cover and continue cooking for 15 to 20 minutes over low heat. Vegetables should still be somewhat crisp. The yield is 4 servings.

SPRING VALLEY LEMON FLAVORED CHICKEN SALAD

4 chicken breasts, cooked and
  diced
8 dashes lemon-pepper

Juice from 3 or 4 whole lemons
8 ribs celery chopped
Mayonnaise

Cook chicken breasts and dice into bite size pieces. Combine with remainder of ingredients; refrigerate until chilled.

WALNUT HILL CHINESE CHICKEN

3 half chicken breasts (total 1¼ pounds)
2½ tablespoons soy sauce
¾ cup chicken broth (condensed)
3 tablespoons vegetable oil
1½ cups snow peas

1½ cups sliced mushrooms
1 cup ¼ inch celery slices
1 medium onion cut in wedges (1/16 inch wedges)
¼ cup green pepper strips
½ cup walnuts

Take spine off of snow peas. Cut and clean all vegetables and place in refrigerator for two or more hours. This will make them stay crispy. Remove skin and bone from chicken and cut in strips. Toss with 1½ tablespoons of soy sauce. Set aside the remaining tablespoon of soy sauce. Combine chicken broth with 2 tablespoons of cornstarch. Heat 1 tablespoon of oil in a skillet and fry chicken until lightly brown around 5 to 6 minutes. Remove chicken and add remaining oil to skillet. When oil is hot add all vegetables and cook over medium heat for 5 minutes. Add broth mixture, chicken, and walnuts, bringing to a boil. Be sure to add remaining soy sauce to broth. Serve at once over rice.

"Let's barbecue a narrow headed yard walker!"

WOODBERRY OVEN BARBECUED CHICKEN

One fryer cut in pieces
6 tablespoons catsup
6 tablespoons brown sugar
Juice of 2 lemons
2 teaspoons paprika
Dash of red pepper
½ teaspoon salt

4 tablespoons Worcestershire
  sauce
8 tablespoons water
2 teaspoons prepared mustard
2 teaspoons chili powder
Dash garlic salt

Combine all ingredients and simmer until blended. Salt and pepper chicken pieces. Dip each piece in sauce and place in aluminum foil lined pan. Pour remaining sauce over chicken. Cover completely with foil. Cook in oven at 450 degrees for 15 minutes. Reduce heat to 350 degrees and cook about 1 hour and 15 minutes. The yield is 8 servings.

CALHOUN COUNTY CORNISH HENS WITH WILD RICE STUFFING

4 Cornish hens, about 1
  pound each
2 teaspoons salt
1 box fast cooking long grain
  and wild rice

One 5 ounce jar or can
  mushrooms
½ cup butter or margarine

Wash hens and pat dry. Rub cavities with salt and set them aside. Cook rice to package directions adding drained mushrooms when done. Stuff hens with rice and mushrooms. Place stuffed hens in large baking dish. Melt butter in saucepan and pour over hens. Cover loosely with foil. Bake 1 hour in 350 degree oven. Remove foil. Baste with drippings and continue baking for ½ to 1 hour, basting frequently.

BIRDTOWN DOVE CASSEROLE

12 doves
Salt and pepper
All-purpose flour
½ cup shortening
One 10¾ ounce can cream of
  mushroom soup

½ cup milk
½ cup red wine
½ cup chopped celery
1 tablespoon chopped onion
1 tablespoon chopped parsley

Salt, pepper, and flour doves. Brown in shortening in skillet. Place browned doves in casserole dish. Combine remaining ingredients and pour over doves. Cover and bake at 350 degrees for 2 to 3 hours or until tender. Serve with wild rice and long grain rice mixture.

CLARKSVILLE DOVE AU VIN

10-12 doves
Salt and pepper
Flour
6 tablespoons butter
1 cup chopped celery

1 cup chopped onion
1 small green bell pepper,
  sliced
One 10 ounce can consomme
½ cup red wine

Salt and pepper doves. Dredge in flour and brown in butter in frying pan. Place in casserole. Add remaining ingredients. Cover and bake at 350 degrees for 2 hours. Add wine during last 30 minutes. The yield is 4 to 6 servings.

JO'S ROAST GOOSE

1 domestic or wild goose,
   cleaned

Salt and pepper
½ cup melted butter

STUFFING:
2 cups dried apricots, cooked in
   hot water and mashed

2 cups bread cubes
3 tablespoons sugar

PLUM SAUCE:
2 cups orange juice
1 cup plum jam

4 tablespoons apricot brandy

Clean goose well. Cover goose with water in large pan and boil for 15 to 20 minutes. Remove and drain. Salt and pepper goose inside and out. Stuff it with the apricot stuffing. If stuffing is not moist enough add a little water. Put goose in greased roasting pan and cover with melted butter. Roast goose at 350 degrees for 20 to 30 minutes per pound, basting often with melted butter drippings. The goose might require more cooking time depending on how large it is. Be sure to give yourself two or three extra hours cooking time before serving. Combine plum sauce ingredients in a small saucepan and heat until slightly warm and thoroughly mixed. Drain all grease off of goose. Pour the sauce mixture over the goose in the roasting pan 20 minutes before serving. Put back into oven and baste several times with sauce before removing from oven. Sliced goose is great served with remaining sauce.

"I'd go over 40 miles of rough road for Jo's Roast Goose!"

OSCEOLA OVEN BAKED QUAIL

8 quail, salted and peppered
1½ cups white wine
½ cup evaporated milk

1½ cups bread crumbs
1 cup butter
2 eggs, beaten

Marinate the quail in wine overnight. Dip quail in beaten eggs and milk. Roll in bread crumbs. Brown in butter in skillet. Place in baking dish. Cover and bake at 350 degrees for 1½ hours or until tender. The yield is 4 servings.

BOONE COUNTY BAKED TURKEY

One 7 to 10 pound turkey
Salt and pepper

Butter
3 cups water

Thaw turkey completely. Wash and dry. Place in roasting pan with water. Brush turkey with butter. Salt and pepper. Cook covered in 300 degree oven (30 minutes per pound). Baste turkey, using turkey stock, often during course of cooking to tenderize and brown the turkey. Bake and serve with Dressing and Gravy recipes to follow.

DRESSING FOR TURKEY

One recipe for Home Town
  Cornbread prepared and
  baked
One 8½ ounce box corn muffin
  mix (baked)
6-8 slices of white bread,
  toasted and buttered
½ stalk celery chopped fine

1 medium onion chopped fine
½ cup butter or margarine
One 14½ ounce can chicken
  broth
3 to 4 cups chicken or turkey
  broth (freshly baked)
2 to 3 teaspoons poultry
  seasoning

Prepare both kinds of cornbread and bake. Toast bread on both sides after buttering. Chop celery and onion and simmer with ½ cup butter and enough water to cover until tender, about 30 minutes. Break toasted bread into small pieces and mix with cornbread also broken into pieces. Heat all broth and celery onion mixture. Add all ingredients and mix thoroughly. Pour into a hot greased iron skillet or into greased baking dishes. Bake at 350 degrees for 45 minutes or an hour. Bake until lightly browned. Serve with turkey and all the trimmings.

GIBLET GRAVY

Turkey giblets, chopped
2 cups giblet stock
1 cup water
2 or 3 boiled eggs, chopped

3 tablespoons flour
3 tablespoons vegetable oil
2 ribs celery

Boil turkey neck and giblets with celery ribs in 6 cups salted and peppered water. Make a paste of flour and vegetable oil and lightly brown in skillet. Slowly add giblet stock and water, allowing to thicken. Add giblets and eggs. Add more stock until you have the desired thickness and amount. (Be sure to remove the turkey neck and celery ribs from stock before using.) Serve with Boone County Baked Turkey.

COUNTRY ROASTED TURKEY

One 14 to 16 pound turkey
½ cup melted butter or
  margarine
1 tablespoon salt
½ teaspoon pepper
2 teaspoons seasoned salt
1 teaspoon ground poultry
  seasoning
1 teaspoon garlic powder

½ teaspoon ground ginger
1 teaspoon paprika
¼ teaspoon cayenne pepper
¼ teaspoon dried basil
¼ onion
1 piece of celery
1 cup water
1 piece of apple (optional)

Clean turkey and dry; put turkey neck, giblets, and liver in saucepan. Cover with water and simmer until fully cooked. Brush turkey with melted butter. Mix together all dry ingredients and rub thoroughly into inside and outside of turkey. Place onion, celery and apple inside cavity of turkey. Place turkey breast side up in roasting pan. Add water and cover. Bake for 3 to 4 hours at 350 degrees or until tender. If turkey is not evenly browned, remove cover for last ½ hour and lower temperature to 300 degrees. You can use a turkey roasting bag. Just follow directions on bag for roasting. Giblets and broth from giblets will make a delicious gravy. The yield is 14 to 16 servings.

LODGE CORNER APRICOT WILD DUCKS

3 large wild ducks
Salt
Pepper
½ cup melted butter
2 cups dried apricots (cooked
    in hot water)

2 cups bread cubes
2 tablespoons sugar
1 cup orange juice
½ cup currant jelly
3 tablespoons apricot brandy

Cover ducks in a large pan with water and boil for about 15 minutes. Remove ducks and dry thoroughly.

Season the ducks inside and out with salt and pepper. Mix together apricots, bread cubes, sugar, and enough hot water to make mixture moist. Stuff ducks with apricot mixture. Place ducks in roasting pan and pour melted butter over top. Cover ducks and roast in 350 degree oven for 1½ to 2 hours or until tender.

In saucepan, combine the orange juice, jelly, and apricot brandy. Warm sauce. Pour sauce over ducks 15 minutes before serving. Baste ducks until serving time. Sauce makes great gravy to serve over ducks.

PECKERWOOD WILD DUCK IN RED WINE GRAVY

4 wild ducks
1 cup flour
1 teaspoon paprika
½ cup vegetable oil

1 onion, quartered
1 apple, quartered
1 orange, quartered
Salt and pepper

RED WINE GRAVY:
One 10¾ ounce can cream of
    mushroom soup
One 10¾ ounce can of beef
    bouillon soup
1 cup of sherry or dry red wine
½ cup sliced mushrooms

½ teaspoon salt
1 teaspoon paprika
1 teaspoon parsley flakes
Dash of Worcestershire sauce
1 soup can water

Mix the paprika, salt and pepper into the flour. Dredge the ducks with the flour mixture and lightly brown them in a skillet with the cooking oil. Stuff each duck with a quartered piece of onion, apple and orange. Place the ducks in a covered roasting pan. Combine all the gravy ingredients in sauce pan and heat until soup has dissolved. Pour gravy over the ducks in the roaster and bake at 350 degrees for 3 to 4 hours or until tender. The yield is 8 servings.

"You can eat like a HOG but you don't have to look like one."

Eat all you want of these low calorie foods.

Asparagus	Squash
Broccoli	Tomato
Brussels Sprouts	Turnip Greens
Cabbage	Watercress
Carrots	Water
Cauliflower	Coffee
Celery	Tea
Chicory	Club soda
Collards	Clear Broth
Cucumber	Bouillon
Escarole	Consomme
Green Beans	Sugarless lemonade
Kale	Spices
Lettuce	Herbs
Mushrooms	Vinegar
Mustard Greens	Lemon
Parsley	Lime
Spinach	

Fruits
and
Vegetables

APPLE ANNIE'S BAKED APPLES

4 medium cooking apples　　**Cinnamon**
2 teaspoons margarine　　**4 teaspoons brown sugar**

　　Wash and core the apples. Place ½ teaspoon margarine, 1 teaspoon brown sugar and sprinkle with cinnamon. Place in greased casserole dish. Bake at 350 degrees for 45 minutes. The yield is 4 servings.

COTTON PLANT CANTALOUPE WITH PORT WINE

　　Cut off top of cantaloupe, scoop out melon meat, carving meat into balls. Place melon balls back into cantaloupe shell and fill and with chilled port wine. Makes an excellent appetizer. Use one melon per person.

CURRIED FRUIT FARMINGTON

1 teaspoon curry powder　　**One 16 ounce can pears,**
½ cup butter, melted　　　**drained**
1 cup packed brown sugar　**One 16 ounce can cherries,**
One 16 ounce can peaches,　**drained**
**　drained**　　　　　　　　**One 15½ ounce can pineapple**
One 16 ounce can plums,　　**chunks, drained**
**　drained**

　　Combine all ingredients. Bake at 350 degrees for one hour in greased baking dish.

BROILED GRAPEFRUIT HALVES

½ grapefruit per person　　**Brown sugar**

　　Sprinkle brown sugar on grapefruit half. Broil for 5 minutes. This accompanies ham or pork.

FRIED HOME GROWN GREEN TOMATOES

4 green tomatoes　　　　**Salt and pepper**
1 cup cornmeal　　　　　**Vegetable oil**

Slice tomatoes ⅛ inch thick. Dip each slice in seasoned cornmeal. Fry in hot oil until browned on both sides. Drain excess grease on paper towels. The yield is 4 to 6 servings.

ASPARAGUS CASSEROLE ASHDOWN

Two 10¾ ounce cans　　　**1 cup shredded mild Cheddar**
**　mushroom soup**　　　　　**　cheese**
Two 10½ ounce cans　　　**2 cups bread cubes**
**　asparagus**　　　　　　　**3 ounces slivered almonds**
4 thinly sliced boiled eggs

Heat juice from asparagus in saucepan and add soup. Toast enough buttered bread slices to break up in bread cubes to measure 2 cups. Layer asparagus, boiled eggs, Cheddar cheese, bread cubes, and almonds in greased casserole dish. Pour soup mixture over each layer. Bake at 350 degrees for 40 minutes.

"Feedin' time!"

ELLIE MAE'S QUICK PICKLED BEETS

VEGETABLES

**One 16 ounce can diced or
sliced beets
½ cup sugar**

**½ cup white vinegar
¼ to ⅓ medium onion
(chopped)**

Mix all ingredients in small saucepan and simmer for 30 minutes to 1 hour or until liquid cooks down. Liquid should only cover beets.

FRENCH FRIED BELL PEPPER RINGS

**2 large green peppers
¼ cup milk**

**1 egg
¼ cup flour**

Slice peppers in ¼ inch rings. Mix egg, milk and flour, stir well. Dip pepper slices into mixture and place in hot vegetable oil. Fry until browned. Drain. Serve while hot. The yield is 4 servings.

KING'S BAKED BARBECUE BEANS

**½ to 1 pound pork sausage
1 large onion
One large 2 pound can, or two
15 ounce cans pork and
beans**

**¾ cup packed brown sugar
3 or 4 dashes hot pepper sauce
¼ to ½ cup hot barbecue sauce
¼ diced bell pepper (optional)**

Brown sausage in skillet, after breaking up with fork into small pieces. Add large onion and simmer. When onion is clear, add other ingredients and simmer on top of stove or in oven for ½ hour.

BROCCOLI AND CHEESE CASSEROLE

3 tablespoons vegetable oil
⅔ cup chopped celery
¼ cup chopped onion
1 package frozen broccoli or
    fresh broccoli (steamed)
One 8 ounce jar cheese spread
1 cup quick cooking uncooked
    rice

One 10¾ ounce can cream of
    chicken soup
¾ cup milk
Salt and pepper to taste
¼ cup shredded Cheddar
    cheese

Sauté celery and onion in oil for one to three minutes. Mix all ingredients together in large bowl and pour into large baking dish. Sprinkle cheese over top and bake 45 minutes at 350 degrees.

BROCCOLI AND CORN CASSEROLE

1 package frozen chopped
    broccoli (cooked)
One 17 ounce can cream style
    corn
One tablespoon diced white
    onion

2 eggs (beaten)
1 tablespoon butter
Salt to taste
Shredded Cheddar cheese
    (enough to cover top)

Prepare broccoli according to directions on the package and drain. Mix with remainder of ingredients. Top with shredded cheese. Bake at 350 degrees for one hour. The yield is 6 servings.

ORIENTAL BROCCOLI

Two 10 ounce packages frozen
    broccoli
2 tablespoons margarine

¼ cup chopped water chestnuts
1 diced pimento
1 tablespoon lemon juice

Cook frozen broccoli to package directions. Drain and set aside. Melt margarine, add chestnuts, pimento and lemon juice. Heat. Serve over hot cooked broccoli. The yield is 4 servings.

MONTICELLO MARINADED CARROTS

2 pounds raw carrots
1 medium green bell pepper - sliced thin
1 medium onion - sliced and ringed
¾ cup vinegar
One 10¾ ounce can tomato soup
½ cup vegetable oil
1 cup sugar
1 teaspoon prepared mustard
1 teaspoon Worcestershire sauce
Salt and pepper to taste

Peel carrots and slice in ¼ inch round slices. Cook in water till barely tender. Drain and cool. Slice bell pepper in thin slices. Slice and ring onion.

Mix all ingredients to marinade and pour over vegetables. Refrigerate overnight. Serve at room temperature. Remove from marinade. Save marinade and use it for French dressing on salads.

COUSIN SHONNA'S CORN SOUFFLÉ

2 eggs, separated
One 17 ounce can cream style corn
2 tablespoons flour
1 teaspoon sugar
1 teaspoon salt

Separate 2 eggs. Combine beaten egg yolks with the can of cream style corn, flour, sugar, and salt. Fold in stiffly beaten egg whites and pile lightly into buttered baking dish. Set in pan of hot water and bake at 350 degrees for 40 to 50 minutes, or until knife inserted in center comes out clean.

CORNING FRIED CORN

8 ears tender white corn
2 tablespoons sugar
2 teaspoons salt
2 tablespoons flour
1 teaspoon pepper
½ cup cold milk
4 tablespoons margarine or butter

Cut corn from cob, scraping each cob to milk it. Combine remaining ingredients. Melt butter in pan and add corn mixture. Cook slowly, stirring constantly for at least 30 minutes. This can scorch easily so watch it carefully.

RAVENDEN ROASTED CORN

6 large ears yellow corn with shucks
Butter

Salt and pepper
Foil
Paper towels

Clean corn, reserve shucks. Butter, salt, and pepper each ear of corn. Wrap each in cornshucks, then in wet paper towel and finally in foil. Place on barbeque grill for 20 minutes, each side. The wet towel and foil seals in the moisture and crispness of each ear.

HOT OUT THE OVEN EGGPLANT CASSEROLE

1 large eggplant
1 large chopped onion
½ cup chopped celery
One package of butter crackers (crushed)
1 cup milk

½ cup shredded Cheddar cheese
2 eggs, boiled and chopped
2 eggs, beaten
½ cup margarine
Salt and pepper to taste

Peel and cube eggplant. Cook in water until tender. Drain and mash. Sauté onion and celery in margarine until tender, but not brown. Mix all ingredients together. Top with a few cracker crumbs and a little cheese. Bake at 350 degrees for 40 minutes in a greased glass baking dish.

"Polynesian Porker"

GREEN BEANS POLYNESIAN

One 16 ounce can French style
  green beans
One 10½ ounce can mushroom
  soup

One 3 ounce can chow mein
  noodles
¼ cup slivered almonds

Combine green beans, soup and almonds. Place in casserole dish. Sprinkle with chow mein noodles. Bake at 300 degrees for 30 minutes.

SNAPPIN EASY FRENCH STYLE GREEN BEANS

Two 16 ounce cans French
  style green beans

1 cup bottled Italian salad
  dressing

Simmer for 30 minutes or until dressing flavor is absorbed.

HARRISBURG HUNGARIAN CUCUMBERS

One 8 ounce carton sour cream
6 tablespoons vinegar
6 tablespoons sugar

12 green onions, sliced
4 cucumbers, peeled and sliced
3 teaspoons salt

Peel and slice cucumbers. Salt and allow to stand for 1 hour. Squeeze out liquid and add remaining ingredients.

PEA RIDGE CASSEROLE

One 10 ounce can cream of
  mushroom soup
One 14 ounce can artichokes,
  chopped
One 16 ounce can tiny green
  peas
1 cup shredded sharp cheese

One 8 ounce can sliced
  mushrooms, drained
1 teaspoon Worcestershire
  sauce
½ cup milk
One 10 ounce package potato
  chips, crushed for topping

Mix all ingredients, top with potato chips. Bake for 30 minutes at 350 degrees, uncovered.

FRESH PURPLE HULLED PEAS & HOG JOWL

1 pound purple hulled peas
½ pound smoked hog jowl (can use ham hock or salt pork)

1 small onion, chopped
Salt and pepper to taste

Wash and cover peas with water. Bring to boil. Add hog jowl, onion, salt and pepper. Cook slowly for 2-4 hours or to desired tenderness.

COMMANDER'S POTATOES

3 pounds Idaho potatoes
1 cup vegetable cooking oil
4 cloves chopped garlic

½ cup butter
2 teaspoons chopped parsley
Salt

Wash, peel and cut potatoes in small cubes. Rinse and drain. Fry in oil until golden brown, remove and set aside to drain on a paper towel. Sauté garlic in butter, add potatoes and parsley. Salt and toss together until potatoes are well covered in garlic butter. The yield is 6 to 8 servings.

GRANNY'S CREAMED POTATOES

4 large or 5 medium white or red potatoes
¼ teaspoon salt

½ cup dairy vegetable blend, cream or canned milk
¼ cup butter or margarine

Peel potatoes and cut in small pieces. Add salt and add only enough water to cover the potatoes. Cover and cook over medium heat for about 20 minutes or until tender. Water should cook down. Whip potatoes with electric mixer. Add butter and dairy vegetable blend. Continue whipping potatoes until they are smooth and creamy.

POLK COUNTY POTATO CASSEROLE

8 potatoes
Salt to taste
Pepper to taste
1½ cups shredded cheese:
  Cheddar, rat trap or American

2 bunches green onions
¼ cup margarine
One 8 ounce carton sour cream

Boil eight potatoes. When done; cool, peel, and grate. Chop the green onions and sauté in margarine. Mix all ingredients together and pour into greased casserole dish. Bake for 45 minutes at 375 degrees.

FAIRFIELD BAY SPINACH OYSTER CASSEROLE

Two 10 ounce packages frozen
  chopped spinach
2 medium onions, chopped fine
1 cup margarine
1 jar of mushrooms
2 tablespoons Worcestershire
  sauce

Two 10¾ ounce cans cream of
  mushroom soup, undiluted
½ cup grated Parmesan cheese
Buttered bread crumbs
Salt and pepper to taste
Oysters

Cook spinach by the package directions and drain well. Sauté onions in margarine, add spinach and seasonings. Combine soup, oysters, Worcestershire sauce and spinach mixture. Place in an uncovered 2 quart casserole. Sprinkle the top with bread crumbs and cheese. Bake at 350 degrees for 30 minutes.

GARDEN SQUASH CASSEROLE

5 to 6 medium yellow squash
4 tablespoons butter or
  margarine
¼ teaspoon salt
½ package butter crackers,
  crushed (four or five large
  wafer crackers)

2 eggs, slightly beaten
½ cup American or Cheddar
  cheese (shredded)
½ of an 8 ounce carton sour
  cream
⅓ cup chopped onion
2 teaspoons sugar

Slice and prepare squash. Add onion, squash, 2 tablespoons butter, salt, and enough water to cover the ingredients in a saucepan. Boil until squash is done. Drain and add all other ingredients. Mix well and pour into greased casserole dish. Bake in 350 degree oven for 30 to 45 minutes. Top should be lightly browned.

GREENLAND ACORN SQUASH

Green acorn squash, ½ per
  person
4 tablespoons butter

⅔ cup brown sugar
1 tablespoon rum

Prepare acorn squash by slicing squash in half. Remove and discard seeds. Place cut side down in ½ inch water in a shallow dish. Bake at 350 degrees for 45 minutes. Turn and fill with creamed butter, sugar and rum sauce. The yield is 2 servings.

SOUR CREAM AND SAUSAGE SQUASH CASSEROLE

½ cup sour cream
1 cup shredded sharp cheese
1 tablespoon butter
1 teaspoon salt
½ teaspoon paprika

1 tablespoon chopped chives,
  or green onion tops
1 egg yolk beaten
1 pound pork sausage
¼ to ½ cup fine bread crumbs

Cook squash and drain. Cook sausage over low heat, crumble well. Combine drained squash, sour cream, cheese, butter, salt, paprika, chives and crumbled sausage. Stir in beaten egg yolk. Pour into greased baking dish and sprinkle top with fine bread crumbs. Bake at 350 degrees for 30 minutes.

SUNRISE SQUASH AND SAUSAGE CASSEROLE

3 medium yellow squash, sliced
½ pound regular pork sausage
½ cup fine bread crumbs or
   cracker crumbs
⅓ cup shredded Cheddar
   cheese

1 egg, beaten
¼ teaspoon salt
¼ teaspoon pepper
4 tablespoons margarine,
   divided
1 onion, chopped

Brown sausage slowly in small skillet. Drain and set aside. Cook squash and onion in a small amount of salted water. Cook until tender and drain. Add bread or cracker crumbs (reserving 1 tablespoon for top). Add cheese, egg, salt, pepper, and two tablespoons of margarine. Add sausage and mix well. Spoon into a greased casserole. Top with remaining crumbs and dot with 2 tablespoons margarine. Bake at 375 degrees for 20 minutes or utnil brown. Makes 4 servings.

SUMMER VEGETABLE CASSEROLE

3 small yellow summer squash,
   sliced
1 medium zucchini, sliced
1 small white onion, sliced
1 tomato, sliced

2 tablespoons grated Parmesan
   cheese
½ teaspoon seasoned salt
½ teaspoon basil
½ teaspoon thyme

Place all sliced vegetables in greased large baking dish and mix well with all other ingredients. Place in oven for 20 to 25 minutes at 350 degrees or microwave on full power for 8 to 10 minutes.

CAROL ANNE'S SWEET POTATO CASSEROLE

3 cups mashed sweet potatoes
¼ cup butter

½ to ¾ cup sugar
3 teaspoons vanilla

TOPPING FOR SWEET POTATO CASSEROLE:
1 cup brown sugar
1 tablespoon flour

⅓ cup butter
1 cup chopped nuts

Mix ingredients for casserole and put into buttered baking dish. Mix ingredients for topping together and sprinkle on top of potatoes. Bake 1 hour at 325 degrees.

SWEET POTATOES IN ORANGE HALVES

12 orange halves
4 sweet potatoes
1 cup white sugar
1 teaspoon salt
¼ cup brown sugar

⅛ cup orange juice
1 teaspoon grated orange peel
3 tablespoons butter
¼ teaspoon nutmeg
1 tablespoon vanilla

Hollow orange halves, reserve pulp. Bake sweet potatoes, peel and cream. Add other ingredients, including pulp. Mix and fill orange shells with sweet potato mixture. Place in buttered pan. Bake for 30 minutes at 325 degrees. The yield is 12 servings.

MISSISSIPPI COUNTY TURNIP GREENS AND HAM HOCK

4 large bunches tender young
  turnip greens
1 ham hock
1 tablespoon sugar
2 teaspoons salt

Pepper
4 tablespoons bacon drippings
1 quart water
1 hot pepper, optional

Wash greens. Pick stems out and discard. Place greens in large pot and cover with water. Add ham hock, bacon drippings and seasonings. Cover and cook until tender.

YODELING YAMS

½ cup butter
½ cup molasses

Two 1 pound cans yams

Melt butter in pan. Stir in molasses and syrup from yams. Stir for 2 minutes until blended and boiling. Place yams in pan. Continue to cook over low heat until glazed, about 15 to 20 minutes. Baste and turn occasionally. The yield is 8 servings.

Meats

BULL SHOALS BEEF BURGERS

1 pound ground lean beef
¼ cup finely chopped onion
1½ tablespoons shortening
½ cup evaporated milk

1 teaspoon salt
⅛ teaspoon pepper
½ cup ketchup

Brown meat and onion in shortening. Stir and break up meat with a fork. Pour off excess grease. Stir into mixture the evaporated milk, salt, and pepper. Cook and stir over low heat until mixture thickens. Remove from heat and stir in catsup. Spoon meat mixture onto hamburger buns.

"Let's Get Greasy' Round The Mouth"

CHEESY BEEF ROLLS A LA CARLISLE

1½ pounds ground beef
2 tablespoons barbecue sauce
¼ cup bread crumbs
½ teaspoon salt
1 egg

1 cup shredded sharp Cheddar
   cheese or processed cheese
¼ cup dry bread crumbs
¼ cup chopped green pepper
2 tablespoons water

Mix together meat, bread crumbs, egg, salt and barbecue sauce. After mixed well, pat meat mixture into 14 by 8 inch rectangle on foil or waxed paper. Combine cheese, bread crumbs, green pepper and water, sprinkle mixture over meat. Roll up jelly roll fashion beginning at narrow end. Chill several hours or overnight. Slice meat roll into six or seven slices. Bake in shallow pan at 350 degrees for 25 to 30 minutes. The yield is 6 servings.

DES ARC PEPPER STEAK

1 large round steak (cut in inch
   strips 2 inches long)
¼ cup vegetable oil
1 clove garlic
2 cups green pepper cut in one
   inch pieces or strips
¼ teaspoon pepper

1 teaspoon salt
¼ teaspoon ginger
1 can consommé (10¾ ounces)
2 tablespoons cornstarch
1 tablespoon soy sauce
½ cup coarsely chopped onion

Heat oil over medium heat in skillet. Brown meat in hot oil with minced garlic added. When brown drain off excess oil and add chopped onion, green pepper, salt, pepper, ginger, 1 can of consommé thickened with cornstarch and seasoned with soy sauce. Cook all ingredients for 3 minutes or until the sauce turns clear. Serve over rice.

GLENDA'S FLANK STEAK MARINADE

2 flank steaks
3 cloves garlic (crushed)
1 teaspoon ground pepper

⅔ cup soy sauce
½ teaspoon hot pepper sauce
½ cup vermouth

Mix marinade sauce and marinate steaks 1 to 2 hours. Broil steaks in oven 4 minutes on each side. Slice the steak when done in thin diagonal slices.

HAMBURG GOULASH

¾ or 1 pound hamburger meat
½ large onion chopped
⅛ teaspoon black pepper
¼ teaspoon salt
One 14½ ounce can tomatoes

3 tablespoon vegetable cooking
oil
8 ounce package Italian style
rotini
Parmesan cheese

Brown hamburger meat and chopped onion in vegetable oil until slightly brown. Drain off excess grease. Add pepper, salt, can of tomatoes with juice. Mash tomatoes with fork or chop with knife. Set the meat mixture aside. Cook the rotini according to package directions. When done drain and add to meat sauce. Sprinkle with Parmesan cheese. May use more or less pepper, salt and cheese, according to taste.

I'm so hungry I could eat the side out of a running steer!

MAMA SPECK'S TUFOLI

2 packages of Tufoli noodles
(hard to find) or Manicotti
noodles

Boil until tender, drain. Place in cool water. Set aside. Drain before stuffing.

SPINACH STUFFING:

½ pound sausage
1 onion, chopped
Two 10 ounce packages of
frozen chopped spinach,
cooked
¾ cup crushed butter crackers

3 eggs, beaten
⅔ cup Parmesan cheese
½ teaspoon thyme, sage,
marjoram
Salt and pepper

Sauté sausage and onion. Combine with cooked spinach, cheese, crackers, eggs and seasonings. Stuff into cooked noodles.

MUSHROOM SAUCE:

Six 6 ounce cans mushroom
sauce or gravy

Pour over stuffed tufoli noodles. Bake in a covered dish for 40 minutes at 350 degrees.

TOMATO SAUCE:

½ pound sausage
1 garlic clove, minced
One 6 ounce can sliced
mushrooms
1 onion, chopped
One 10 ounce can cream of
mushroom soup

One 8 ounce can tomato sauce
½ teaspoon dry basil
¼ teaspoon sugar
One 10 ounce can beef bouillon

Sauté onion and sausage. Add remaining ingredients. Simmer for 1 hour. Spoon sauce over cooked stuffed tufoli noodles just before serving. Sprinkle with Parmesan cheese.

MEATBALLS IN MUSHROOM SAUCE

One 12 ounce package medium
noodles
½ cup stuffing mix
2 teaspoons instant onion (may
use fresh)
½ cup milk
1 pound ground beef
1 egg

1 teaspoon Worcestershire
sauce
2 tablespoons butter
One 10 to 12 ounce can
mushroom gravy
¼ cup light cream (evaporated)
½ teaspoon dill weed

Boil water and cook noodles according to directions. Drain and set aside.
In medium bowl combine stuffing, onions, and milk. When soft, add beef,
egg, and Worcestershire. Mix well with fork. Shape into 2 dozen meatballs.
Heat butter in skillet and brown meatballs. Stir in gravy, cream, and dill.
Simmer covered 10 to 15 minutes. Serve on noodles.

For Cocktail Meatballs: roll meatballs into bite sizes. Cook and serve in
chafing dish spearing with toothpicks. Forget the noodles.

PERFECT ROAST

1 large beef roast
Salt

Pepper

Preheat oven to 450 degrees. Salt and pepper roast and place in uncovered pan. Cook 5 minutes per pound for rare; 6 minutes per pound for
medium; and 7 minutes per pound for well-done. After cooking time has
elapsed turn oven off and do not open for 2 hours. It's perfect!

ROGER'S MOTHER'S SMOTHERED LIVER

1 pound tender beef liver
1 cup all-purpose flour
Seasoned salt
1 medium onion thinly sliced in
rings

4 tablespoons margarine
Black pepper
¼ cup hot water

Salt and pepper each piece of liver and roll in flour. Sauté in melted
margarine until lightly brown on both sides. Place onion rings over the top of
the liver and pour in the hot water. Cover pan and simmer over low heat for
10 to 15 minutes or until liver is tender. Add more water if you need more
gravy.

STUFFED PEPPERS DEVALLS

6 medium green peppers
⅓ cup chopped onion
1 pound ground beef
2 tablespoons oil or margarine
2 cups of cooked fresh
    tomatoes or one 1-pound can

¾ cup precooked rice
2 tablespoons Worcestershire
    sauce
Salt and pepper
1 cup shredded American
    cheese

Prepare green peppers by cutting off the tops and cleaning out the seeds and membranes. Cook the green peppers in boiling salted water for 4-5 minutes. Lay out to drain, then salt insides and lay aside. Brown meat and onion in oil. Add all other ingredients except cheese. Salt and pepper to taste. Cover and simmer until rice is almost tender around 6 minutes. Add cheese. Stuff peppers and turn open side up in greased baking dish. Bake uncovered around 350 degrees for 25 to 30 minutes. Sprinkle with cheese if desired. The yield is 6 servings.

SHERWOOD ENGLISH PRIME RIB

Prime rib or standing rib
2 tablespoons Worcestershire
    sauce
1 teaspoon paprika

Salt
Pepper
Rock salt

Season prime rib with Worcestershire sauce, salt, pepper, and paprika. Rub the seasonings into the meat. Put a layer of rock salt in the bottom of a heavy roasting pan. Pour just enough water over rock salt to lightly dampen it. Place the prime rib in the standing rib position onto the rock salt. Cover the prime rib completely with rock salt and dampen it with water just as before. Do not cover. Place in oven preheated to 500 degrees. Roast meat 15 minutes per pound. Remove from oven when done. Remove salt crust from meat. It will be very hard and must be broken carefully away from meat. This process does not allow shrinkage and traps juices in meat. Serve ½ pound per serving.

SPANISH BEEF

1 pound ground beef
1 large onion
1 piece of celery
2 tablespoons of chili powder
Two 8 ounce cans tomato
  sauce
Two 8 ounce cans water

One 17 ounce can yellow cream
  style corn
One 3 ounce jar stuffed olives
One 8 ounce package noodles
½ pound shredded American or
  Cheddar cheese
Salt and pepper

Brown ground beef with chopped onion and sliced celery. Add chili powder, tomato sauce, corn and olives. Prepare noodles according to directions on the package. Drain and place noodles in large flat baking dish. Pour ground beef mixture over noodles. Top with cheese. Bake until bubbling hot at 350 degrees or for 30 minutes.

STEAK DIANE

Four 6 ounce beef fillet steaks,
  ½ inch thick
Salt and pepper

2 tablespoons butter
½ cup cognac

SAUCE: Combine and heat.

4 tablespoons butter
4 tablespoons chopped green
  onions
2 tablespoons chopped parsley

4 tablespoons sherry or wine
2 tablespoons Worcestershire
  sauce
2 tablespoons steak sauce

Season steaks. Melt butter and sauté steaks over low heat for 2 minutes on each side. Pour sauce over steaks and continue cooking until bubbling. Add cognac, ignite it. The yield is 4 servings.

SWEDEN POT ROAST

4 pounds beef pot roast (chuck, brisket, flank)
1 teaspoon nutmeg
1 teaspoon cinnamon
½ teaspoon ginger
2 teaspoons salt
½ teaspoon pepper

2 tablespoons shortening
2 onions, sliced
1 clove garlic, diced
½ cup brown sugar
½ cup red wine or vinegar
¾ cup water
4 bay leaves

Combine nutmeg, cinnamon, ginger, salt, pepper, and rub into the meat. Heat pressure cooker and add shortening. Brown meat well on all sides. Add onion, garlic, brown sugar that has been dissolved in wine, water and bay leaves. Close cover securely. Place pressure regulator on vent pipe and cook 40 minutes with pressure regulator rocking slowly. Let pressure drop of its own accord. This will be a very tender meat with a different flavor.

VILONIA VEAL PARMESAN

4 veal cutlets, ¼ inch thick (1 pound)
⅓ cup buttery cracker crumbs
⅓ cup grated Parmesan cheese
¼ teaspoon salt
1 beaten egg with 1½ tablespoons water

One 8 ounce can tomato sauce
½ teaspoon dried, crushed oregano
½ teaspoon sugar
⅛ teaspoon onion salt
3 ounces mozzarella cheese
dash pepper

Combine crumbs, cheese, salt, and a dash of pepper. Combine egg and water. Dip veal in egg mixture then in crumb mixture. Place veal in 12 x 8 x 2 inch greased baking dish. Bake uncovered for 20 minutes at 400 degrees. Turn and bake 15 to 25 minutes more. Combine tomato sauce, oregano, sugar, and onion salt. Heat to boiling, stirring frequently. Pour over meat. Top with mozzarella cheese and return to oven to melt cheese, 2 to 3 minutes more. The yield is 4 servings.

BOONEVILLE BARBEQUED PORK ROAST

5 to 6 pound pork loin roast or other lean pork roast
10 ounce jar apple jelly

½ cup hickory smoked barbecue sauce

Salt roast and place flat side up in covered roasting pan. Roast in slow over (325 degrees) until well done. Cook until roast is tender about 45 to 50 minutes per pound. When roast is tender, mix together apple jelly and hickory smoked barbecue sauce. Baste roast with sauce and heat uncovered in low (300 degree) oven until lightly browned.

"Oh no, not him!"

CULPEPPER PORK CHOPS

6 pork chops
2 tablespoons all-purpose flour
1 teaspoon salt
dash of pepper
2 tablespoons vinegar
1 green pepper (cut in ⅛ inch rings)

¼ cup ketchup
1 small onion (cut in thin slices)
Two 15½ ounce cans pineapple chunks
½ cup pineapple syrup

Coat pork chops with flour, salt and pepper. Brown in greased skillet, with rest of flour mixture. Combine other ingredients and pour over chops. Cover and simmer 45 minutes.

"Eatin' high on the hog."

CRANBERRY-PINEAPPLE CHOPS

4 large smoked pork chops
2 tablespoons vegetable
  cooking oil
All-purpose flour
Salt
Pepper

One 16 ounce can jellied
  cranberry sauce
½ cup crushed pineapple
1 tablespoon grated orange rind
¼ cup water

Salt and pepper smoked chops and roll in flour. Brown chops in heated vegetable cooking oil. Mix other ingredients in skillet and add chops. Cover and simmer for 1 hour or until chops are tender when pierced with a fork. The yield is 4 servings.

"Cram it in with both hands and stomp it down with both feet."

MARVEL GLAZED PORK CHOPS

6 loin pork chops, ¼ to ½ inch thick
One 17 ounce can apricots

1 teaspoon salt
1 tablespoon steak sauce
½ teaspoon whole cloves

Combine syrup from apricots, steak sauce and salt in saucepan. Cook 10 to 15 minutes over medium heat until the sauce thickens a little. Arrange pork chops in shallow uncovered baking dish. Baste both sides with sauce and bake at 400 degrees. Turn chops once after 45 minutes, brush again with sauce. Stick cloves into apricots and place around chops. Bake for 30 minutes longer until tender. The yield is 3 servings of 2 chops each.

MORRILTON MINCEMEAT STUFFED PORK

3 pound boneless pork
One 9 ounce package condensed mincemeat
4 tablespoons cider vinegar

3 tablespoons orange marmalade
½ teaspoon salt
¼ teaspoon pepper

Preheat oven to 350 degrees. Mix 2 tablespoons of vinegar and the mincemeat in a bowl. Make a 1½ inch wide opening through the middle of the pork loin. Pack the opening with the mincemeat mixture. Place the pork in a roasting pan. Combine the remaining ingredients and pour over the pork. Bake uncovered for 1½ hours or until a meat thermometer inserted 1 inch deep registers 170 degrees. Cover and remove from oven. The yield is 8 servings.

PIGGOTT PORK CHOPS AND ARKANSAS GROWN RICE

4 to 6 pork chops (seasoned to taste)
1 cup raw Arkansas grown rice

1 package dry onion soup
One 2.5 ounce can mushrooms
3 cups water

Brown seasoned pork chops. Set aside. In large greased baking dish put raw rice. Sprinkle with onion soup mix saving 1 tablespoon for later. Sprinkle on mushrooms and then evenly cover with 3 cups of boiling water. Place the chops on top and sprinkle them with remaining soup mix. Tightly cover with foil and bake at 350 degrees for about 45 minutes.

For freezing - only cook about 30 minutes and put in freezer after cool. When ready to serve, it will finish cooking by the time it heats throughly.

LITA'S BARBECUED LEG OF LAMB

One 4 to 5 pound leg of lamb
1 cup catsup
½ cup bottled hickory smoked barbecue sauce

2 heaping tablespoons brown sugar
½ cup water
Salt and pepper to taste

Place salted and peppered leg of lamb in large baking pan with lid. Bake slowly in a 325 degree over for 5 to 6 hours or until meat is tender and comes loose from the bone easily. Mix all other ingredients together and set aside. When leg of lamb is done, coat or pour barbecue sauce over it and bake another 20 minutes. This is a great meat dish to serve for your favorite company!

Hmmm . . .

127

PORTIONS OF EACH FOOD GROUP

CALORIE ALLOWANCE PER DAY	FAT	BREAD	MILK	FRUIT	VEGETABLE	MEAT
800	0	1	1½	2	1	5
900	0	2	1½	3	1	5
1000	0	2	2	3	1	5
1100	0	3	2	4	1	5
1200	1	4	2	4	1	5
1300	3	4	2	4	1	5
1400	3	5	2	3	1	6
1500	4	5	2	4	1	6
1600	5	6	2	4	1	6
1700	5	6	2½	4	1	6
1800	5	6	2½	4	2	7
1900	5	7	2½	5	2	7
2000	5	7½	2½	5	2	8
2100	6	7½	2½	6	2	8

(See chart on page 58)

Miscellaneous

"Sunny side up with the yellow running way out . . . !"

EGGS BENEDICT

4 poached eggs
4 slices Canadian bacon, fried

4 English muffin halves
Hollandaise sauce

Place slice of Canadian bacon on English muffin half. Place poached egg on top. Cover with Hollandaise sauce. The yield is 2 servings.

EAST TEXAS EGGS

6 tortillas, warmed
9 scrambled eggs
1½ cups refried beans, heated

1½ cups guacamole
One 8 ounce jar salsa sauce
One 8 ounce carton sour cream

On each tortilla place a helping of scrambled eggs, refried beans, and guacamole. Roll the tortilla around the layers. Top with salsa sauce. Garnish with sour cream. Serve hot! The yield is 6 servings.

FARMHOUSE BACON, GRITS AND EGGS

1 cup quick grits
4 cups water
½ cup butter or margarine
1 cup shredded Cheddar
  cheese

1 pound fried bacon
6 eggs
½ cup milk
Salt to taste

Cook grits in water. Add butter, cheese and 2 beaten eggs. Pour into casserole dish. Layer half the crumbled bacon over mixture. Mix eggs and milk. Pour over grits mixture. Sprinkle top with remaining crumbled bacon. Bake at 350 degrees for 50 minutes. Serve immediately while still hot. The yield is 6 to 8 servings.

GARDEN FRESH ZUCCHINI QUICHE

1 uncooked pastry shell
2 small zucchini, sliced thin
1 ounce Parmesan cheese,
   grated
4 ounces Gruyere cheese,
   shredded

4 eggs, beaten
1½ cups heavy cream
½ teaspoon salt
⅛ teaspoon nutmeg
⅛ teaspoon pepper

Preheat oven to 375 degrees. Place cheeses in unbaked pie shell, top with zucchini slices. Pour remaining mixture of eggs, cream and seasonings over zucchini. Bake in preheated oven for 45 minutes or until custard is set. The yield is 4 to 6 servings.

SPRINGHILL CHEDDAR SCRAMBLED EGGS

12 eggs
½ cup milk
2 cups Cheddar cheese
2 teaspoons finely chopped
   green onions

1 teaspoon salt
¼ teaspoon pepper
4 tablespoons butter

Beat eggs. Heat butter in skillet. Mix eggs with other ingredients and pour into 10 inch skillet over low heat. Scramble until cooked. The yield is 6 servings.

QUICK QUICHE

1 frozen pie shell
1 cup shredded Swiss cheese
8 slices fried bacon
3 eggs, beaten

1 cup milk
1 tablespoon chopped onion
Salt and pepper

Bake pie shell in preheated oven at 350 degrees for 10 minutes. Crumble bacon and combine with remaining ingredients. Pour into prebaked pie shell. Bake at 350 degrees for 30 to 40 minutes. The yield is 6 servings.

BERDIE B.'S BREAD PUDDING

PUDDING:

6 bread slices,toasted
3 eggs
1 cup sugar
1 cup milk

1 teaspoon cinnamon
½ teaspoon nutmeg
½ teaspoon salt
Raisins (optional)

Sauce: for topping
2-3 tablespoons butter
2 tablespoons all-purpose flour
¾ cup milk

¾ cup brown sugar
Juice from ½ lemon

Combine all ingredients and bake at 350 degrees until firm but moist. Combine ingredients for sauce in saucepan and cook over low heat until thickened. Serve over bread pudding.

CHERRY VALLEY ICE CREAM

½ gallon vanilla ice cream
Two 16 ounce cans bing
   cherries
1 cup chopped pecans

½ pint whipped cream
2 dozen crushed macaroons
½ cup sherry

Allow ice cream to soften. Drain juice from cherries. Pour sherry over cherries and let soak. While ice cream softens, combine all ingredients, including sherry and ice cream. Refreeze.

"Ice cream, ice cream, we all scream for ice cream!"

CREAM DE MENTHE PARFAIT

Vanilla ice cream   **Fresh strawberries**
Cream de Menthe, green

Spoon ice cream into parfait glasses. Dribble Cream de Menthe over ice cream. Repeat layers until parfait glasses are filled. Top with a fresh strawberry, and freeze until served. This is as pretty as a new baby pig!

"Pretty as a new baby pig!"

DOWN HOME CUSTARD ICE CREAM

½ cup all-purpose flour   **2 cups sugar**
2 tablespoons vanilla   **1 quart sweet milk**
6 eggs separated   **2 cans evaporated milk**

Mix all ingredients except egg whites and mix well. Cook over low heat until mixture thickens. Beat egg whites and fold into hot mixture. Cool. Freeze in electric freezer. Great to add fresh bananas, peaches, or strawberries for a different taste.

HOMEMADE CHOCOLATE ICE CREAM

One 14 ounce can sweetened
   condensed milk
⅔ cup chocolate syrup

2 cups (1 pint) whipping cream,
   whipped
½ teaspoon vanilla

In large bowl, stir together sweetened condensed milk and syrup. Fold in whipped cream. Pour into aluminum foil-lined 9 x 5 inch loaf pan: cover. Freeze 6 hours or until firm. Scoop ice cream from pan or remove from pan, peel off foil and slice. Return leftovers to freezer. This makes a great frozen pie, with ice cream mixture poured into a prepared chocolate flavored ready-crust. Makes two pies.

RASPBERRY-LEMON SOUFFLE

1½ cups milk
½ teaspoon salt
6 eggs separated
¾ cup sugar
Two envelopes unflavored
   gelatin

Two 10 ounce packages frozen
   raspberries in syrup, thawed
2 lemons
1 cup whipping cream

With wire whisk, beat egg yolks with milk, salt, and ½ cup sugar until blended. Place mixture in large saucepan. Sprinkle gelatin over egg yolk mixture and let stand 1 minute to soften gelatin. Cook over low heat until gelatin dissolves and mixture thickens, about 30 minutes, stirring frequently. Remove from heat. Pour ½ mixture into a bowl and leave ½ in the saucepan. Set both halves aside. Blend raspberries in blender or processor until puréed. Strain to remove seeds. Pour all of raspberry mixture over yolk mixture in bowl and refrigerate for 45 minutes, stirring often.

Grate 1 teaspoon lemon peel and squeeze ¼ cup lemon juice. Pour over egg yolk mixture in pan and refrigerate for 30 minutes, stirring occasionally. In the meantime, prepare a collar for a 1½ quart souffle dish. Tear off a piece of waxed paper long enough to wrap around the outside of the souffle dish. Fold it in half lengthwise and secure with a string so that at least 3 inches of waxed paper stands up above rim of dish. Beat egg whites in bowl until soft peaks form gradually adding ¼ cup sugar. Continue to beat until sugar is dissolved and stiff peaks form. Divide in half. Beat whipping cream until soft peaks form. Divide in half. Fold in half of the egg whites and half of the whipped cream into the lemon mixture. Fold in the other half of the egg whites and half of the whipped cream into the raspberry mixture. Alternate layers of lemon mixture and raspberry mixture in prepared souffle dish. With a spoon or spatula cut through the mixture to marbleize. Cover and refrigerate for at least 4 hours. The yield is 12 to 16 servings

SODA POP ICE CREAM

2 cans sweetened condensed milk   **48 to 50 ounces of any flavor soda**

Blend together condensed milk and soda. Freeze in your electric ice cream freezer according to directions. Great ice cream and easy too!

"Larrupin' good!"

TINY GELATIN SQUARES

Three 3 ounce packages flavored gelatin (any flavor)   **4 envelopes unflavored gelatin**
4 cups boiling water

Mix all gelatin in boiling water until gelatin is completely dissolved. Pour into 13 x 9 inch baking pan and chill until firm. Cut ½ to 1 inch squares. Great for quick snack.

BERTHA'S BREAD AND BUTTER PICKLES

9 pounds cucumbers
(before cut)
8 small white onions

2 green peppers shredded
½ cup salt

SYRUP:
5 cups sugar
1½ teaspoons turmeric
½ teaspoon ground cloves

2 teaspoons mustard seed
1 teaspoon celery seed
5 cups vinegar

Select crisp fresh cucumbers, do not pare. Slice cucumbers crosswise in paper thin slices. Slice the onions thin and cut peppers fine. Food processors are great for this. Mix salt with the three vegetables and pack mixture in pieces of cracked ice. Cover with lid. Let stand 3 hours and then drain thoroughly.

Mix syrup and pour over sliced cucumber mixture. Place over low heat and stir occasionally. Heat to scalding, but do not boil. Heat until they all change color. Pour in jars and seal.

BRADLEY COUNTY GREEN TOMATO RELISH

6 quarts small green tomatoes,
quartered
3 quarts medium onions,
quartered
1 quart medium-size hot green
chili peppers, chopped (use
canned if you like)

1 large sweet red pepper,
seeded and chopped
10 teaspoons salt
8 cups sugar
4 cups cider vinegar
4 cups water

Combine all ingredients in a large enamel pan, bring to boil, and then simmer until onions are clear 20 to 25 minutes. Ladle into sterilized pint jars and seal. The yield is 12 pints.

CHARLESTON CHUTNEY

1 cup raisins, simmered for two minutes and drained
1 pound can apricot halves, drained and coarsely chopped
Two 18 ounce jars pear preserves

One 16 ounce jar peach preserves
Two 8 ounce jars orange marmalade
One 3 ounce jar pinhead onions
1/3 teaspoon powdered sugar
3/4 cup steak sauce

Mix ingredients. Let stand for 24 hours. Place into sterilized jars. Spoon into canned peach halves, heat and serve with meats. The yield is 2 quarts.

GARLAND GARLIC PICKLES

1 gallon sour pickles
1½ boxes pickling spice
3 tablespoons olive oil

5 pounds white sugar
6 garlic buttons

Slice pickles into 3/4 to 1 inch slices. Place layer of pickles into bottom of jar, sprinkle layer of sugar, then layer of spices, and a garlic button. Repeat layers. Add olive oil on top. Seal jars. Turn jars every day for 8 days. Open after 6 weeks.

HAYDEN'S RELISH

1 gallon ripe tomatoes
1 quart chopped onions
1 gallon chopped cabbage
7 large bell peppers, chopped
3/4 cup salt

1 quart red wine vinegar
6 cups sugar
1/2 box pickling spices in cheesecloth bag
6-8 hot peppers, chopped

Mix first four ingredients in a large pan. Sprinkle the salt over the mixture. Let stand for two hours. Drain. Cover with red vinegar. Add the sugar and the pickling spices. Bring mixture to a boil and add the hot peppers. Cook for only 15 minutes. Pour into sterilized jars. Serve with blackeyed peas. The yield is 11 to 12 pints.

"Short sweetenin'"

PEACH ORCHARD MARMALADE

20 peaches, sliced
2 oranges, sliced
Juice of 2 lemons

Sugar
2 cups walnuts

Mix one cup of peaches per one cup sugar. Let set 4 hours. Combine with orange slices and lemon juice. Cook slowly for 1 hour. Add walnuts just before removing from stove. Pour into sterilized jars. Seal with melted parafin.

FRENCHMAN'S BAYOU REMOULADE SAUCE

½ cup chopped celery
¼ cup chopped parsley
¼ cup chopped onion
1 cup vegetable oil
2 teaspoons Worcestershire
  sauce
¼ cup malted vinegar

½ cup hot creole mustard
¼ cup horseradish
¼ cup paprika
2 teaspoons salt
1 teaspoon ground black
  pepper
1 quart mayonnaise

Combine all ingredients. Refrigerate. This can be served on cold boiled shrimp, tomatoes, lettuce, on lobster or crabmeat or as a salad dressing. The yield is 1½ quarts.

FRESH BUTTER HOLLANDAISE SAUCE

½ cup fresh butter
2 tablespoons all-purpose flour
2 egg yolks

½ cup boiling water
Juice of 1 lemon
Salt and pepper

Mix all ingredients except water. Cook until thick. Add water just before serving.

GARLIC-BUTTER SAUCE

¼ cup butter, melted
¼ teaspoon crushed garlic
¼ teaspoon salt

¼ teaspoon sugar
1½ teaspoons lemon juice
4-5 drops hot pepper sauce

Combine all ingredients. Spoon over any broiled fish fillets. This is especially good over pan-fried trout or perch.

"Blubber up to the table!"

SPECK'S MARCHAND DE VIN SAUCE

1½ cups butter (no substitute!)
⅔ cup fresh mushrooms, chopped
⅔ cup green onions, finely chopped
1 cup onion, finely chopped
4 tablespoons minced garlic

4 tablespoons flour
1 teaspoon salt
¼ teaspoon pepper
1½ cups beef broth
1 cup red wine
Dash cayenne

Sauté mushrooms in melted butter. Add green onions, onion, and garlic. Sauté until tender. Add flour, salt, pepper and cayenne. Blend in beef broth and wine. Simmer over low heat, stirring constantly until well blended and thickened. Serve over beef fillet. Excellent! The yield is 4 cups.

STRAWBERRY BUTTER

One 8 ounce package strawberries, thawed and drained

One cup soft butter
3 tablespoons powdered sugar

Blend all ingredients in a food processor, blender or mixing bowl. Serve with homemade biscuits, bagels, popovers, or any other favorite bread. If butter separates from strawberries you may want to add more powdered sugar.

SUMMER TOMATO SAUCE

2½ pounds fresh ripe summer tomatoes
1 medium red onion, finely chopped
1 pressed garlic clove
4 or 5 sprigs fresh parsley

2 or 3 leaves fresh basil
Salt to taste
½ cup freshly grated Parmesan cheese
Freshly ground black pepper

Simmer onions, tomatoes (peeled) with garlic. Add remaining ingredients. Do not add water or oil. Cover and simmer for 1½ to 2 hours. Serve over thin spaghetti adding only freshly grated Parmesan cheese and fresh ground pepper. The yield is 4 servings.

TARTARE SAUCE

2 cups mayonnaise
1 small onion chopped extra fine

½ cup chopped sweet pickles
1 tablespoon lemon juice

Mix all ingredients and refrigerate. This is excellent with fish of all kinds. The yield is 3 cups.

"WHITE" SAUCE

¼ cup mayonnaise
2 tablespoons flour
¼ teaspoon salt

Dash of pepper
1 cup milk

Combine first four ingredients, cooking slowly, gradually adding milk. Stir constantly until thickened. For a variation add 1 cup shredded Swiss or Cheddar cheese. Serve over vegetables, crepes or chicken. The yield is 1¼ cups.

CRISPY GRANOLA

2 cups uncooked oats
1 cup coconut
1½ cups wheat germ
1½ cups almonds

1 teaspoon salt
1 can condensed milk
¼ cup vegetable oil
1½ cups raisins

Mix all ingredients together exept raisins. Spread on top of waxed paper on large cookie sheet. Bake for 1 hour at 300 degrees. Stir every 15 minutes. When done mix in raisins. Cool completely before putting into sealed container.

NACHOS

One 17 ounce package of
  tortilla chips
One 8 ounce package shredded
  Cheddar cheese
One 4 ounce jar of jalapeño
  peppers, sliced crosswise
  into pieces

1 chopped onion (optional)
One 16 ounce can refried beans
  (optional)

Place tortilla chips spaced apart on cookie sheets. On top of each chip place cheese and piece of pepper. Place under broiler just long enough to melt cheese.

For a variation: on the chip, place refried beans, onions, cheese, and pepper in that order. Place in hot oven long enough to melt cheese and heat beans. Serve hot.

Pastries and Pies

JOHNNY APPLE CRISP

4 cups sliced cooking apples
  (may use a large jar of apple
  sauce)
1 tablespoon lemon juice
⅓ cup all-purpose flour
1 cup quick or old fashioned,
  uncooked oats

½ cup brown sugar
½ teaspoon salt
1 teaspoon cinnamon (optional)
⅓ cup melted butter or
  margarine

Place apples or apple sauce in buttered baking dish. Sprinkle with lemon juice. Combine dry ingredients: add melted butter. Mix until texture is crumbly. Sprinkle crumb mixture on top of apples. Bake in 350 degree oven for 30 to 40 minutes. Great warm or cold. Good topped with whipped cream. The yield is 6 servings.

"An apple a day keeps the Doc away!"

WASHINGTON APPLE SQUARES

2½ cups all-purpose flour
1 tablespoon sugar
½ teaspoon salt
1 cup shortening
1 egg yolk and enough water to make ⅔ cup

1 cup crushed corn flakes
8 apples sliced thin
2 or 3 tablespoons butter
1 cup sugar
1 egg white
1½ teaspoons cinnamon

ICING:
1 cup powdered sugar
1 teaspoon vanilla
1 tablespoon butter

2 tablespoons milk, water or orange juice

Mix flour, and 1 tablespoon sugar, and salt in food processor or blend by hand. Cut in shortening then add egg yolk and enough water to make ⅔ cup. Mix liquid with other ingredients. Roll out dough like pie crust in two 15½ inch x 10½ inch rectangles. Place bottom crust on cookie sheet. Sprinkle with crushed corn flakes. Place sliced apples on top of corn flakes, sprinkle with sugar mixed with cinnamon. Dot with butter. Roll out other crust and place on top. Spread lightly with butter and then with beaten egg white. Bake 1 hour at 350 degrees.

Mix icing and spread over crust. Cut in squares.

"Hoggin' it down"

SWEET HOME
TINY CHOCOLATE GLAZED CREAM PUFFS

1 cup water
½ cup butter
¼ teaspoon salt

1 cup all purpose flour
4 eggs

In a saucepan, combine water, butter and salt. Heat until boiling. Remove from heat and stir in flour. Add eggs, one at a time, beating after each. Drop by heaping teaspoons onto greased cookie sheet and place in preheated oven (375 degrees). Bake for 25-30 minutes. Let cool. Slice off top half.

FILLING FOR CREAM PUFFS

3 cups whipping cream
⅓ cup powdered sugar

⅓ cup cocoa
¼ cup almond flavored liqueur

Beat all ingredients at medium speed until soft peaks form. Fill cooled cream puffs.

CHOCOLATE GLAZE FOR CREAM PUFFS

Six 1 ounce squares semisweet
   chocolate
2 tablespoons butter

2 tablespoons milk
1 tablespoon light corn syrup

Combine ingredients in double boiler over low heat. Stir frequently until smooth. Spoon over tops of cream puffs.

HAMBURG FRESH STRAWBERRY PIE

1 cup lemon lime soft drink
1 cup sugar
2 heaping tablespoons
  cornstarch

Few drops red food coloring
1 pint fresh strawberries

Mix sugar and cornstarch together until well blended. Add liquid and food coloring. Cook over medium heat until thick. Add one pint of fresh strawberries. Pour into a cookie pie crust or a regular pastry crust and top with cool whip or sweetened whipped cream. Refrigerate until firm.

HERMITAGE STRAWBERRY PARFAIT PIE

One 3 ounce package
  strawberry gelatin
1 cup hot water
½ cup cold water

1 pint vanilla ice cream
1 cup sliced fresh strawberries
1 baked 9-inch pastry shell
Whipped cream to trim

Dissolve gelatin in hot water. Add cold water, and stir. Add a pint of vanilla ice cream cut in six chunks; stir until melted. Chill until mixture mounds slightly when dropped from a spoon. (20 to 30 minutes) Gently fold in one cup sliced fresh strawberries. Pour into baked, cooled 9-inch pastry shell. Chill until firm, 20 to 25 minutes. Trim with whipped cream and berries.

BECKY JO'S SWEETHOME POTATO PIE

2 cups mashed sweet potatoes
1 cup sugar
1½ cups evaporated milk
3 eggs
½ teaspoon salt

½ teaspoon cinnamon
½ teaspoon nutmeg
1 teaspoon vanilla
2 tablespoons margarine

Blend all ingredients together and pour into unbaked pie shell. Bake at 350 degrees for 60 minutes or until knife is tested in center of pie and comes out clean.

BLACK ROCK BOTTOM PIE

CRUST:
20 ginger snaps, crushed   **6 tablespoons melted margarine**

Combine crushed ginger snaps and butter and press into 10 inch pie pan. Bake in 300 degree oven for 10 minutes.

CUSTARD FILLING:
1 tablespoon unflavored gelatin   **Dash of salt**
1¾ cups milk   **4 egg yolks**
½ cup sugar   **1 tablespoon water**
1 tablespoon cornstarch

Mix unflavored gelatin and water; set aside. Scald milk adding sugar, cornstarch and salt. Stir in beatened egg yolks. Cook slowly over double boiler until thickened. Stir in gelatin. Divide mixture in half.

CHOCOLATE FILLING:
2 squares unsweetened   **1 teaspoon vanilla**
  chocolate

Melt chocolate with vanilla; add to half of custard mixture, stir to blend. Pour over cooled crust. Set aside.

RUM FILLING:
4 egg whites, stiffly beaten   **½ cup sugar**
⅛ teaspoon cream of tartar   **1 tablespoon light rum**

Beat egg whites and cream of tartar. Add sugar slowly. Fold into custard adding rum. Spoon over cooled chocolate layer. Refrigerate to chill.

WHIPPED CREAM TOPPING:
½ pint whipping cream   **Grated unsweetened chocolate**
1 tablespoon sugar

Whip cream and sugar. Spread on pie. Top with grated chocolate. Refrigerate overnight unless made early in the day. It needs time to "set up" before serving. The yield is 6 to 8 servings.

DELIGHTFUL PECAN PIE

4 egg whites at room
   temperature
1 cup sugar
1¾ teaspoons baking powder
2 teaspoons vanilla

2 cups soda crackers, coarsely
   broken
¾ cup chopped pecans
1½ to 2 cups whipped cream or
   substitute

Whip egg whites until soft peaks form. Gradually add sugar and baking powder until sugar is dissolved and firm peaks form. Add vanilla. Gently fold in crackers and pecans. Pour into greased 9 inch pie pan. Bake at 350 degrees for 1 hour. Cool upside down. When cooled, top with whipped cream and chopped pecans.

"Happy as a pig in the mud in the sunshine!"

FRENCHPORT COCONUT PIE

3 eggs
1½ cups sugar
½ cup margarine at room
   temperature
One 3½ ounce can flaked
   coconut

1 teaspoon vinegar
1 teaspoon vanilla
1 unbaked pie shell (9-inch)

Soften margarine to mixing consistency and combine with remaining ingredients. Pour into pie shell and bake 1 hour at 350 degrees.

OLD JENNY LIND BANANA ALMOND PIE

8 ounces cream cheese
¾ cup sugar
⅓ cup all-purpose flour or 3
  tablespoons cornstarch
¼ teaspoon salt
2 cups milk
3 slightly beaten egg yolks

2 tablespoons butter or
  margarine
1 teaspoon almond extract
3 sliced bananas
Non-dairy whipped topping or
  sweetened whipped cream

In saucepan combine sugar, flour, and salt; gradually stir in milk and slightly beaten egg yolks. Blend well. Cook over medium heat stirring constantly. Cook until mixture thickens. Remove from heat, add butter, cream cheese, and almond flavoring. Blend. Place half the sliced bananas in pie crust. Use a cookie crust pie crust or a regular pastry pie crust. Pour half cream filling over bananas. Place other half of bananas over filling and pour remaining cream mixture on top of bananas. Top with cool whip or sweetened whipped cream. May save some of the bananas to decorate top of pie. Refrigerate until ready to serve.

PEACH ORCHARD CREAM PIE

¾ cup sugar
⅓ cup flour
¼ teaspoon salt
2 cups milk
4 slightly beaten egg yolks
2 tablespoons butter or
  margarine

1 teaspoon vanilla
4 large fresh peaches sliced
One 9-inch baked pastry shell
Cool whip or whipped cream

Combine sugar, salt, and flour in large saucepan. Mix these ingredients thoroughly. Add milk, beaten egg yolks, and butter. Blend well. Cook stirring often, to keep from burning on bottom of pan. Cook till mixture is pudding consistency. Remove from heat and add vanilla. Cool and then pour half of mixture in pie shell. Place peaches on top of cream filling. Pour remaining cream filling over peaches. Top with cool whip or sweetened whipped cream. This pie would also be great topped with meringue.

PICKENS PEACH PARFAIT PIE

3½ cups sliced peaches,
   sweetened or 1 No. 2½ can
   peaches
One 3 ounce package lemon or
   peach flavored gelatin

½ cup cold water
1 pint vanilla ice cream
1 baked 9-inch pastry shell
½ cup whipping cream,
   whipped or non-dairy topping

If using fresh peaches let them stand about 15 or 20 minutes after mixing with sugar. Drain fresh or canned peaches, reserving syrup.

Add water to syrup to make 1 cup and heat to boiling. Add gelatin; stir until dissolved. Add cold water. Cut ice cream into 6-pieces, and add to hot liquid. Stir until melted. Chill until mounds slightly when dropped from a spoon. (about 20 minutes) Fold in peaches. Pour into baked pie shell.

Chill for several hours for firm filling. Trim with whipping cream and sliced peaches.

PINEAPPLE SUPREME PIE

One 12 ounce can condensed
   milk
One 15½ ounce can crushed
   pineapple
1 cup chopped nuts

¼ cup lemon juice
One 12 ounce size carton
   non-dairy whipped topping
2 drops yellow food coloring
Graham cracker crust

Combine milk, pineapple, nuts and lemon juice. Add non-dairy whipped topping and food coloring. Pour into graham cracker crust. Chill. At Christmas time, red and green candied cherries can be added to make it look more festive.

"Keep your eyes on them pies while I say grace!"

POOR MAN'S PECAN PIE

4 eggs (slightly beaten)
2 cups sugar
1 cup milk
1½ cups dark or light corn
   syrup

1½ cups uncooked oats
½ cup butter or margarine
1 teaspoon salt
1 cup coconut
Two 9 inch pie crusts (unbaked)

Mix all ingredients in order as given. Pour into unbaked pie crust. Bake 1 hour in 350 degree oven. Makes two 9 inch pies.

ROSEBUD RAISIN PIE

2 cups raisins
2 cups boiling water
½ cup sugar
2 tablespoons all-purpose flour

½ cup chopped pecans
2 teaspoons grated lemon peel
2 tablespoons lemon juice

Cover raisins with boiling water. Cook until tender, around 5 minutes. Mix together sugar and flour. Stir constantly as you slowly pour sugar and flour mixture into boiling raisins. Remove from heat and stir in lemon juice and grated lemon peel. Pour into an unbaked pie shell and add a pastry top. Bake at 450 degrees for 30 to 40 minutes.

CRUMBLIN GRAHAM CRACKER CRUST

1½ cups graham cracker
   crumbs

½ cup butter (melted)
¼ cup sugar

Mix all three ingredients and pat into pie shell. Great with our sour cream cheese cake.

"Common Doin's"

DAISEY'S COOKIE PIE CRUST

1 cup all-purpose flour
½ cup butter or margarine

¼ cup powdered sugar
1 teaspoon vanilla

Melt butter over low heat in saucepan. Remove from heat and add flour, powdered sugar, and vanilla. Press into pie pan. Bake in 350 degree oven until lightly brown, 10 to 15 minutes. Great for cream pies or the fresh fruit pies.

PRATTSVILLE PERFECT PIE CRUST

SINGLE PIE CRUST:
1½ cups all purpose flour
½ teaspoon salt
4 to 6 tablespoons cold ice
    water

½ cup shortening

DOUBLE PIE CRUST:
2 cups all purpose flour
1 teaspoon salt

⅔ cup shortening
5 to 8 tablespoons cold water

If you have a food processor, use it for making pastry. Follow these same directions using a food processor. Mix or sift together flour and salt. Cut in shortening with a pastry blender or a fork until pieces are about the size of small peas. Sprinkle ice water over mixture and blend until dough sticks together. Mix with fingers and separate dough into two balls. Roll out on lightly floured board. When dough is rolled to desired size gently roll onto rolling pin and transfer dough to pie plate. If you have made only a single pie crust you do not separate dough before rolling out.

LEMON BLUEBERRY TART

1½ cups blueberries, rinsed
5 tablespoons grated lemon
    rind
1 cup lemon juice
½ cup melted butter

6 eggs, beaten
1 cup sugar
10 inch partially baked tart
    shell, 1 inch deep
Powdered sugar

Preheat oven to 400 degrees. Combine lemon juice, lemon rind, and butter. Add eggs and sugar. Stir well. Pour into prebaked tart shell and bake until brown. Place blueberries over warmed filling, pressing slightly. Dust with powdered sugar when cool. These can also be made into small individual tarts. The yield is 8 servings.

Penny Pinchin'
"One Dish Meals"

TUCKERMAN BEEF POTATO PIE

1 pound ground beef
1 cup fresh or frozen onion
One 8 ounce can tomato sauce
½ teaspoon salt
¼ teaspoon black pepper

½ teaspoon celery salt or
   seasoned salt
3 cups mashed potatoes
1 cup shredded Cheddar
   Cheese

Preheat oven at 375 degrees. In skillet sauté ground meat with onion. Cook until meat loses its red color. Drain off fat if necessary. Stir in tomato sauce, salt, black pepper, and seasoned salt. Spoon into 1½ quart shallow baking dish. Spread mashed potatoes on top. Sprinkle with shredded Cheddar cheese. Bake for 30-35 minutes uncovered, or until cheese is melted and casserole is bubbly.

"More than plenty"

CHICKALAH CHICKEN CASSEROLE

2 tablespoons margarine
1 large onion, chopped
8 ounce can chili peppers
1 package frozen tortillas
4 cups cooked, boned and
   diced chicken
2 cups shredded Cheddar
   cheese

One 10½ ounce can enchilada
   sauce
One 10 ounce can cream of
   chicken soup
One 6 ounce can evaporated
   milk
2 cups chicken broth

Saute onions in margarine. Add chili peppers. Layer casserole dish with uncooked tortillas, then chicken, cheese, sautéed onions and chili peppers. Repeat layers. Top with cheese. Combine all liquid ingredients, mixing well. Pour over casserole. Bake uncovered for 1 hour at 350 degrees. This can be made the night before and refrigerated until ready to cook. The yield is 8 servings.

CAMDEN CHICKEN AND BROCCOLI CASSEROLE

5 chicken breast
Two 10 ounce packages frozen
  broccoli, partially cooked
One 10¾ ounce can cream of
  chicken soup
½ teaspoon curry powder
½ cup bread crumbs

⅔ cup mayonnaise
⅓ cup condensed milk
2 tablespoons white wine
1 tablespoon lemon juice
¾ cup Cheddar cheese
3 tablespoons butter

Combine chicken and broccoli. Mix curry, soup, mayonnaise, condensed milk, wine and lemon juice. Pour this mixture over the chicken and broccoli. Sprinkle Cheddar cheese on top, following with bread crumbs. Dot top with butter. Bake at 350 degrees for 45 minutes. The yield is 5 servings.

MILLER COUNTY COUNTRY CHICKEN AND DUMPLINGS

1½ cups all-purpose flour
½ teaspoon salt
5 tablespoons water
Chicken broth
Cooked chicken (removed from
  bone)
1 egg beaten

3 tablespoons shortening
1 tablespoon chopped onion
1 tablespoon chopped celery
1 hard boiled egg (chopped
  fine)
Pepper to taste
Salt to taste

Mix flour and salt together, cut shortening into flour mixture with a fork, blend until like cornmeal. Add water mixed with beaten egg. When well blended divide into 3 parts. Roll out very thin and let sheets of dough dry for 20 minutes. Cut in small strips and drop in broth of chicken which has been cooked tender and removed from the bones. Add to broth 1 tablespoon of chopped onion and 1 tablespoon of chopped celery. Also add chopped egg. Season with salt and pepper. Cook dumplings until tender.

CHICKEN WALDO WITH WHITE RICE

1 cup white rice
4 chicken breasts, halves
One 10¾ ounce can of cream of
   celery, cream of mushroom,
   or cream of chicken soup

Salt and pepper
Parmesan cheese (optional)

Grease pan with oil or margarine. Sprinkle rice into pan. Place chicken breasts on top of rice. Mix water with soup until smooth and pour mixture over chicken and rice. Sprinkle with salt and pepper. Top with Parmesan cheese if desired. Cover and bake at 350 degrees for 1½ hours. Remove cover for another 20 - 30 minutes, allowing chicken to brown. The yield is 2 to 4 servings.

WATER CHESTNUT CHICKEN SPAGHETTI

1 hen, 5 to 6 pounds
1 large onion, chopped
1 large bell pepper, chopped
2 cups celery, chopped
1 large jar pimento, chopped
Two 10¾ ounce cans cream of
   mushroom soup
2 cups chicken broth
8 ounces grated sharp Cheddar
   cheese

1 tablespoon sugar
½ cup margarine
One 16 ounce package thin
   spaghetti
1 teaspoon garlic salt
One 8 ounce can water
   chestnuts, sliced thin
Salt and pepper to taste

Boil hen until tender. Salt and pepper to taste while cooking. Remove bones from hen and chop into bite size pieces. Sauté onion, pepper, and celery in margarine. Cook spaghetti in chicken broth. Mix all ingredients together, place in casserole dish, cover with grated cheese, and bake at 350 degrees until cheese melts. The yield is 6 to 8 servings.

WOLLEY HOLLOW CHICKEN SALAD CASSEROLE

¾ cup mayonnaise
¼ cup water
One 10¾ ounce can cream of
   chicken soup
2 cups diced cooked chicken
2 tablespoons grated onion

½ cup blanched almonds
¼ cup chopped green pepper
1½ cups cooked rice
½ teaspoon salt
4 hard cooked eggs
2 cups crushed potato chips

    Mix mayonnaise, water and undiluted soup together. Add chicken, onion, pepper, slivered almonds, rice, salt, topped with sliced eggs, carefully. Place all in greased casserole topped with crushed potato chips. Bake 30 minutes at 350 degrees. The yield is 10 servings.

PORK AND BEANS CHILI ELDORADO

3 pounds ground chuck
1 medium onion
3 cloves of garlic
1 tablespoon salt
One 10¾ ounce can tomato
   soup

4 cans water in soup can
6 tablespoons chili powder
1 tablespoon cumin
½ teaspoon sugar
1 small can pork and beans

    Brown meat in skillet without grease. Add chopped onion, and garlic. Remove meat and onions from skillet and move into large saucepan. Add all other ingredients and simmer 30 minutes.

ANTOINE LASAGNA

1 pound lean ground beef
1 clove garlic, minced
One 1½ ounce package dry
  onion soup mix
One 6 ounce can tomato paste
1½ cups water
One 8 ounce can tomato sauce
½ teaspoon salt
¼ teaspoon pepper

½ teaspoon sugar
1 teaspoon oregano
½ teaspoon basil
½ pound cooked lasagna
  noodles
½ pound shredded mozzarella
  cheese
1 pound cottage cheese
Grated Parmesan cheese

Brown meat and garlic over low heat in a large deep skillet or saucepan. Cook around 10 to 15 minutes or until lightly browned. Blend in onion soup mix, water, tomato paste, tomato sauce, salt, pepper, sugar, oregano, and basil. Simmer for 15 minutes more, stirring occasionally. Cook lasagna noodles according to package directions. Drain. Grease a baking dish that is 13½ x 8¾ x 1¾ inch. Pour a layer of meat first, followed by noodles, cottage cheese, and mozzarella cheese. Begin the layers again starting with the cottage cheese, mozzarella cheese, noodles and then meat sauce on top. Sprinkle with Parmesan cheese. Bake at 375 degrees for 30 to 40 minutes or until hot.

MR. MAC'S MACARONI AND CHEESE

One 10 ounce package jumbo
  macaroni
Two 10¾ ounce cans
  mushroom soup
Grated onion to taste

1 pound shredded sharp
  Cheddar cheese
1 cup evaporated can milk
Salt, pepper, and paprika to
  taste

Cook macaroni and drain. Mix together mushroom soup, grated onion, evaporated milk, salt, pepper, paprika, and Cheddar cheese. Layer sauce and macaroni in greased casserole dish. Bake at 350 degrees for 45 minutes.

MOCK RAVIOLI MONTICELLO

2 pounds ground beef
2 large onions
3 cloves of garlic
1 teaspoon Italian seasoning
¼ cup Parmesan chesse
2 small packages shell
  macaroni
One 16 ounce can tomato sauce
One 8 ounce can tomato paste

One 4 ounce can sliced
  mushrooms and juice
1 package frozen spinach
4 eggs
One 3 ounce bottle olive oil
¼ cup chopped parsley
Salt and pepper
1½ cups water

Brown ground beef and onion in olive oil. Add seasonings and sauces. Add mushrooms, juice, and water. Simmer for 30 minutes. Prepare spinach according to directions on package. Cook shell macaroni. Mix all ingredients together. Add cheese, eggs and parsley. Place in large baking dish, sprinkle top with cheese and bake at 350 degrees for 30 minutes. The yield is 8 servings.

ANNA'S RICE MUSHROOM CASSEROLE

1⅓ cups packaged precooked
  rice
One 3 ounce can sliced
  mushrooms and liquid
1 cup cold water
¼ cup finely chopped onion

1 teaspoon Worcestershire
  sauce
½ teaspoon salt
2 tablespoons butter or
  margarine

Sauté onion in butter until onion turns clear. Add all other ingredients and pour into greased baking dish. Bake for 45 minutes at 350 degrees.

GRAND PRAIRIE RICE

1 cup uncooked rice
½ cup margarine, melted
1 cup water

One 10 ounce can beef
  consommé
1 package of onion soup mix

Combine ingredients and bake at 400 degrees for 40 minutes in greased casserole dish.

BUD'S CRAB BISQUE

Two 6 ounce packages frozen snow crab meat, thawed
One 11¼ ounce can green pea soup
One 11 ounce can tomato bisque soup
One 14½ ounce can whole tomatoes, chopped
2 fresh tomatoes, chopped
One 5 ounce can evaporated milk
2 ounces whole milk
3 tablespoons butter
⅛ teaspoon cayenne pepper
¼ teaspoon nutmeg
⅛ teaspoon paprika
3 whole, small green onions, chopped
5 springs fresh chopped parsley
Dash of hot pepper sauce
Dash of Worcestershire
Seasoned salt to taste
Salt and pepper
Brandy to taste

Combine all the ingredients and simmer over low heat for 30 minutes. Brandy evaporates quickly, so add more before each new serving. Serve Bud's incredible culinary miracle with a simple salad topped with french-Roquefort dressing and hot buttered french bread. Gulp...Yum...Chomp...Mrphff...Glug...Gorge...Smack...Ummm...More... Um...MMM!!!

"Slurpin' good!"

HAM BONE SOUP

2½ quarts water
1 pound dried beans or lentils
1 meaty ham bone
1 chopped carrot
1 cup chopped celery
Two 8 ounce cans tomato
  sauce with little tomato bits

1 teaspoon Worcestershire
  sauce
½ teaspoon salt
½ teaspoon seasoned salt
¼ teaspoon pepper

Put all ingredients in large heavy pot and simmer, covered for 2 hours or until beans are tender. Stir occasionally. Remove ham bone from soup. Remove any meat from the bone and return it to soup. Remove all fat that floats to top of soup. The yield is 6 to 8 servings.

"Foot stompin' good!"

MERRY'S BEAN SOUP

One 28 ounce can whole
  tomatoes
One 8 ounce can tomato sauce
1 to 2 large onions, minced
3 buds garlic, minced

2 to 3 ribs celery, chopped
1 small bell pepper, chopped
One 2 pound package Great
  Northern Beans
1 pound smoked link sausage

Soak beans overnight. Put all ingredients (except meat) in a large pot (8 to 10 quart size), fill with water. Add: red and black pepper to taste, but no salt. Cook two hours, add salt, if needed. Boil slowly 5 to 8 hours total. The last hour add ham, which has been chopped coarsely and sausage, cut into bite size pieces.

Serve a green salad - garlic bread or Mexican bread. This freezes beautifully! More pepper will be needed after thawing.

MINERAL SPRINGS MINESTRONE

3 tablespoons tomato paste
Two 16 ounce cans tomatoes
Two 13½ ounce cans tomato
  juice
Two 10½ ounce cans beef
  consommé
½ cup white beans
4 tablespoons butter
1 cup frozen English peas
1 cup unpeeled zucchini
1 cup carrots
1 cup potatoes
½ cup celery

2 ounces salt pork
1 medium onion
½ cup leeks
2 bay leaves
Salt and pepper to taste
Garlic salt to taste
Parsley
Basil
Parmesan cheese (on top when
  served)
Garlic
Olive oil

Bring water to boil. Add beans, boil 2 minutes. Remove from heat. Soak in the water for 1 hour. Return to heat and simmer for 1 to 1½ hours. Drain, set aside. Melt butter. Add; seasonings, peas, zucchini, carrots, potatoes, celery. Toss with wooden spoon 2 to 3 minutes until coated with butter.

Fry salt pork with olive oil, drain. Sauté onions and leeks, and tomato paste, thinned with 3 tablespoons water. Add: tomatoes, tomato juice, consommé, salt pork, vegetables. Cook slowly 45 minutes to 1 hour. Add: beans, elbow macaroni, and rice. Cook until tender. Serve with lots of Parmesan cheese on top.

ROMANCE CRAB SOUP

Two 10 ounce cans cream of
  celery soup
One 10 ounce can tomato soup
One 10 ounce can crab soup

One 6 ounce can crabmeat or 1
  cup fresh crabmeat
4 cups half and half
Sherry to taste

Combine and heat. Spike with Sherry and you're ready for romance.

OZARK VEGETABLE SOUP

2 medium soup bones
6 cups water
4 medium or 3 large onions,
  chopped
2 cups chicken broth
Two 1 pound cans tomatoes
1 package frozen mixed
  vegetables
1 cup canned, frozen, or fresh
  cooked lima beans

One 1 pound can cream corn
3 cups celery, chopped
¾ teaspoon pepper
2 teaspoon salt
½ cup okra, cut
1 potato diced
1 cup medium egg noodles

In large heavy soup pan put soup bones, onions, celery, chicken broth, water, tomatoes, salt and pepper. Boil 5 to 7 minutes. Reduce heat and simmer for 1 hour. Remove bones and cool. Remove meat from bones and add to liquid. Add vegetables and simmer for 1 hour. Add noodles and simmer for 20 minutes.

"Boil the pot!"

166

SUZANNA'S SPAGHETTI

1 pound ground beef
2 onions finely chopped
2 cloves of a garlic bulb, minced
Two 16 ounce cans of tomato sauce
One 14 ounce can of whole tomatoes, cut in quarters
4 cups water
One 4 ounce can sliced mushrooms
1 teaspoon oregano
1 teaspoon marjoram
1 teaspoon thyme
2 bay leaves
1 tablespoon of Italian seasoning
2 tablespoons of olive oil (may substitute vegetable oil)
Salt and pepper
One 16 ounce package of spaghetti pasta
Parmesan cheese

Saute ground beef and onion in olive oil until onion is tender. Add remaining ingredients and simmer for 2 hours. Prepare pasta according to package directions. To serve, pour sauce over spaghetti or mix together. Sprinkle with Parmesan cheese. The yield is 6 servings.

JONESBORO SPAGHETTI

1½ pounds hamburger meat
1 medium onion, chopped
1 small bell pepper, chopped
1½ cups ketchup
¾ cup water
2 tablespoons sugar
¼ teaspoon salt
¼ teaspoon pepper
Dash chili powder
8 ounces fresh sliced mushrooms
¼ cup vegetable oil
1 package thin spaghetti

Heat cooking oil in skillet. Add hamburger meat, chopped onion, chopped green bell pepper, and lightly brown. Drain excess oil from skillet. Add other ingredients except mushrooms and simmer over low heat for 30 minutes. Add mushrooms and simmer another 10 to 15 minutes. Prepare spaghetti to package directions and pour desired sauce over each serving.

MOM'S BEST CHICKEN SPAGHETTI

1 cooked chicken, boned and
   cut up
½ cup shredded cheese
½ cup milk
⅓ cup all-purpose flour
¾ cup butter
One 10 ounce package long
   spaghetti

1 onion, chopped
1 bell pepper, chopped
½ cup chopped celery
One 2½ ounce can mushrooms
Chicken broth, seasoned with
   ½ teaspoon salt

Cook spaghetti in chicken broth, seasoned with salt. When spaghetti is done drain broth off and set aside. Sauté onion, bell pepper, and celery in ¼ cup butter. Combine remaining melted butter, milk, flour, and cheese in skillet and cook over low heat until mixture begins to thicken. In large pan mix all ingredients to spaghetti. If dry add a little of the chicken broth to sauce mixture. It may take ¾ to 1 cup of broth. Heat in casserole dish in oven until hot.

PLAIN OL' ITALIAN SPAGHETTI

1 pound ground beef
1 onion chopped fine
2 cloves garlic (minced)
Two 8 ounce cans tomato
   sauce
One 14 ounce can whole
   tomatoes
1 can water
One 4 ounce can mushrooms,
   sliced

2 tablespoons Italian seasoning
1 tablespoon olive oil
1 teaspoon thyme
1 teaspoon oregano
1 teaspoon marjoram
2 bay leaves
Parmesan cheese
1 package of spaghetti

Fry ground beef until brown in olive oil. Add onion and garlic and stir until soft. Add remaining ingredients. Cook slowly for 2 hours. Cook favorite spaghetti and pour sauce over it or mix spaghetti in it. Sprinkle with Parmesan cheese. The yield is 4 to 6 servings.

PORK RIBS SPAGHETTI WITH GRAVELLY GRAVY

6 cans whole tomatoes
  (14 ounce can)
6 cans tomato paste (6 ounce
  can)
¼ to ½ cup sugar
1 tablespoon salt
½ teaspoon pepper (more if
  desired)
Shake oregano across top of
  gravy

teaspoon basil (fresh if
  possible)
4 bay leaves
1 onion, chopped
1 clove garlic, minced
4 to 6 pork ribs
1½ pounds hamburger meat
4 to 5 cups water

Brown pork ribs and hamburger meat with garlic until brown. Mix all other ingredients with meat and cook on low, simmering all day. Great on any Italian dish. You can use less water for thicker sauce.

"On top of spaghetti, all covered with sauce!"

169

ONE DISH MEALS

SPAGHETTI SAUCE WITH J. BENTEN MEATBALLS

SAUCE:

2 large cans whole tomatoes
One 8 ounce can tomato sauce
One 8 ounce can tomato juice
One 6 ounce can tomato paste
2 bay leaves
1 teaspoon oregano
1 teaspoon pepper
2 teaspoons salt

Dash dried celery flakes
Dash dried parsley
Dash sweet basil
1 large onion, chopped
2 whole celery pieces
1 minced garlic clove
3 tablespoons vegetable
  cooking oil

MEATBALLS:

2 pounds ground chuck
2 eggs
¼ cup bread crumbs
2 teaspoons salt

1 teaspoon pepper
Dash parsley
Dash celery flakes
Parmesan cheese

Saute onion and garlic in cooking oil. Add remaining ingredients. Cook over medium heat unitl it bubbles. Combine meatball ingredients and form into meatballs. Brown the meatballs and add to the sauce. Continue cooking at lowest temparture for at least 4 hours. Serve over spaghetti. Top with Parmesan cheese. The yield is 6 servings.

BEST EVER BEEF STEW

½ cup sherry cooking wine
1 clove crushed garlic
3 to 4 pounds lean stew meat
3 stalks celery, chopped
2 onions, chopped
4 or 5 carrots, cut in large
  pieces
4 or 5 potatoes, peeled and cut
  in large pieces

Fresh mushrooms
Salt (seasoned)
2 bay leaves
Pepper (seasoned)
2 tablespoons sugar
1 tablespoon tapioca
3 cups tomato juice
One 8 ½ ounce can English
  peas

Saute meat lightly. Add all other ingredients, except peas and mushrooms. Bake in large roasting pan 4½ hours at 250 degrees. 30 minutes before done add peas and mushrooms.

LONGHORN FAN STEW

2 pounds lean beef, cut in 2
   inch cubes
Water, enough to cover beef
¼ cup vegetable oil
2 bay leaves
Salt and pepper
1 teaspoon soy sauce
3 stalks celery, cut in 1 inch
   strips
1 large onion, cut in quarters,
   then quarters again

4 red potatoes, cut in quarters
½ cup red cooking wine
2 tablespoons Worcestershire
   sauce
½ pound fresh mushrooms, cut
   in half
1 small bunch carrots, cut in 2
   inch lengths
Cornstarch for thicking
1 longhorn fan, optional

Brown beef in oil in skillet. Salt and pepper. Cover with water and cook slowly for at least 1 hour or until tender.

Add remaining ingredients. Continue to cook until vegetables are done. Additional water may be added. Thicken with cornstarch. Serve over fluffy long grain rice. The yield is 4 to 6 servings.

"Stew until meat falls from the horns"

LUXORA CABBAGE STEW

1 pound ground beef
2 medium onions, chopped
½ head medium cabbage,
    coarsely chopped
½ cup celery
One 15½ ounce can kidney
    beans, drained

One 14½ ounce can tomatoes
1 cup water
1 teaspoon salt
¼ teaspoon pepper
1 to 2 teaspoons chili powder

Brown ground meat slowly in its own fat. Drain and mix with all other ingredients in large heavy soup pan. Chop the canned tomatoes. Simmer over low heat for 20 to 30 minutes or until cabbage is slightly tender. Do not over cook. Great served on a cold day with cornbread!

LOCKESBURG BEEF STROGANOFF

1 pound ground beef
1 large onion (chopped)
1 clove garlic
1 teaspoon salt
1 teaspoon pepper
½ cup Cheddar cheese (grated)
4 to 8 ounce can mushrooms
    (sliced)

One 10¾ ounce can mushroom
    soup
1 cup sour cream
One 12 ounce package flat
    noodles, cooked
Sprig of parsley

Brown ground beef and sauté onion until tender. Add seasoning and remaining ingredients. Additional Cheddar cheese can be placed on top. Bake at 350 degrees until bubbling. The yield is 6 servings.

Salads
and
Salad Dressings

ANTIOCH APRICOT GELATIN

Two 3 ounce packages apricot
  gelatin
2 cups hot water
2 cups cold water

One 15¼ ounce can crushed
  pineapple, drained, save juice
2 large bananas, mashed
2 cups miniature marshmallows

TOPPING:
½ cup pineapple juice
½ cup sugar
2 tablespoons flour
2 tablespoons butter

1 egg, well beaten
Two 3 ounce packages cream
  cheese

Dissolve gelatin in two cups of boiling water. Add two cups of cold water. Mix together crushed pineapple that has been drained and mashed bananas. Save pineapple juice for topping. Add the pineapple and bananas to the gelatin. Then stir in marshmallows. When gelatin is firm mix topping and spread on gelatin. Refrigerate until ready to use.

TOPPING: Mix sugar and flour together in small saucepan. Add other ingredients except cream cheese. Cook over low heat until mixture thickens, stirring constantly. When thickened add cream cheese. Spread on gelatin when firmly jelled.

BALD KNOB POTATO SALAD

1 cup salad dressing or
  mayonnaise
3 teaspoons prepared mustard
½ teaspoon celery seed
½ teaspoon salt
⅛ teaspoon pepper

4 cups cubed cooked potatoes
2 hard cooked eggs, chopped
½ cup onion, chopped fine
½ cup celery, chopped fine
½ cup chopped sweet pickle or
  sweet relish

Boil potatoes in jackets and cool. When completely cool, peel and cut into cubes. Combine salad dressing, mustard, celery seed, salt and pepper, and mix well. Add potatoes, eggs, onion, celery and pickle: mix lightly. Chill. The yield is 6 servings.

BERRYVILLE CRANBERRY SALAD

1 package of finely chopped
  cranberries
One 15½ ounce can crushed
  pineapple, drained
1½ cups sugar
2 cups diced or miniature
  marshmallows

1 cup pecans or walnuts
  (chopped)
1 pint of whipping cream
  (whipped)

Combine first five ingredients. Chill overnight. Three to four hours before serving, fold in whipping cream. The yield is 6 servings.

BIBB SALAD

Fresh Bibb lettuce
One 16 ounce can grapefruit
  sections

One 11 ounce can mandarin
  orange sections
Poppyseed dressing

Combine ingredients and toss. Fresh spinach can be substituted for Bibb lettuce. The yield is 4 servings.

CHERRY HILL COLA SALAD

Two 16 ounce cans bing
  cherries
1 cup crushed pineapple
Two 3 ounce packages cherry
  gelatin
One 3 ounce package cream
  cheese

2 cups fruit juice from cherries
  and pineapple (add enough
  water to make 2 cups)
12 ounces of cola
1 cup pecans

Bring to a boil the fruit juice and pour this over the gelatin stirring until completely dissoved. When cool, add cola. Stir and chill in refrigerator until this is partially congealed. Add drained fruit and nuts. Add cream cheese by pinching off small pea size pieces, and adding one at a time. Pour into mold.

CHERRY VALLEY GELATIN SALAD

1 can pie cherries (in water)
1 cup sugar
2 packages raspberry gelatin

1 small can crushed pineapple
(drained)
½ cup pecans

Bring to boil a can of sour pie cherries and liquid (unsweetened cherries). Add sugar and heat. While liquid is hot dissolve gelatin in cherry mixture. Then add a can of crushed pineapple and nuts. Chill until jelled. Top with cream cheese and orange juice.

TOPPING: Whip one 8 ounce package of cream cheese with electric mixer. Mix with one small can of frozen orange juice.

"Fattenin' Day!"

CHRISTMAS SALAD

One 16 ounce can whole
    cranberry sauce
1 cup boiling water
One 3 ounce package
    strawberry flavored gelatin

1 tablespoon lemon juice
¼ teaspoon salt
½ cup mayonnaise
1 apple, diced
¼ cup chopped walnuts

Heat cranberry sauce, strain. Mix liquid, boiling water and gelatin. Stir until completely dissolved. Add lemon juice and salt. Chill mixture until slightly thickened. Add mayonnaise and beat with a beater until fluffy. Fold in reserved berries, apple and nuts. Stir and chill until slightly thickened then put in desired mold.

CRITTENDEN CABBAGE SLAW

1 medium cabbage
1 small onion
1 bell pepper
¾ cup sugar
1 cup vinegar

½ cup vegetable oil
1 teaspoon salt
1 teaspoon celery seed
1 tablespoon prepared mustard

Shred vegetables and mix with sugar. Put in saucepan vinegar, vegetable oil, salt, celery seed, prepared mustard. Boil for 4 minutes. Pour over cabbage mixture immediately. Refrigerate. Cover tightly. Better the next day.

"Tender Green Garden Sass!"

GREENLAND SALAD

1 head chilled Romaine lettuce
2 heads chilled Bibb lettuce
Anchovies
1 clove of a garlic bulb, minced
2 tablespoons of lemon juice
¼ cup olive oil
2 tablespoons red wine vinegar

1 coddled egg
8 drops Worcestershire sauce
½ teaspoon dry mustard
½ cup Parmesan cheese
Salt and pepper
¼ cup croutons

Gently tear lettuce into large pieces. Chill in ice water to maintain crispness. Mix all ingredients in large wooden bowl. Drain lettuce thoroughly and toss with Dressing. The yield is 4 servings.

HOMESTYLE FRUIT SALAD

SALADS

One 15½ ounce can pineapple chunks
2 oranges
1 cup pecans
1¼ cups miniature marshmallows
1 cup whipping cream (whipped)
2 tablespoons flour
2 eggs
½ cup sugar
Coconut (if desired)
Dash of salt

Drain pineapple, place juice in double boiler. Mix sugar, flour, salt and eggs. Pour this mixture into juice and cook until thickened. Stir constantly. Cool mixture. Peel oranges and cut into small pieces. Add pineapple chunks, nuts, and marshmallows. Add all this to cooled sauce. Before serving, add whipped cream and a little coconut.

MANDARIN ORANGE GELATIN

Two 3 ounce packages orange gelatin
1 cup boiling water
1 pint orange sherbet
1 can mandarin oranges - drained
2 cups non dairy whipped topping

Dissolve gelatin in water. Add sherbet and mix well. When partially set, add oranges. Fold in non dairy whipped topping. Pour into 1½ quart dish and refrigerate. The yield is 8 servings.

MARIANA SPINACH SALAD

SALAD:
Two 10 ounce packages fresh spinach
4 hard boiled eggs, chopped
8 strips bacon, fried until crispy then crumbled

DRESSING:
1 cup light vegetable oil
5 tablespoons red wine vinegar
4 tablespoons sour cream
½ teaspoon dry mustard
2 tablespoons sugar
2 teaspoons chopped parsley
2 cloves garlic, crushed
1½ teaspoons salt

Mix dressing at least 6 hours before serving. Toss spinach with desired amount of dressing before serving. Top with bacon and eggs.

179

MARSHMALLOW SALAD

Two 11 ounce cans mandarin
  oranges
One 20 ounce can pineapple
  chunks
Two 6¼ ounce packages
  marshmallows

One 14 ounce package coconut
Two 8 ounce cartons sour
  cream

Drain oranges and pineapple and mix well with all other ingredients. Cover in large container and refrigerate overnight.

"Put the feed bag on!"

ORANGE, PINEAPPLE, CRANBERRY SALAD

2 oranges, quartered
One 8 ounce box strawberry
  gelatin dessert mix
One 15¼ ounce can crushed
  pineapple

1 cup hot water
1 cup chopped celery
1 pound fresh cranberries

Grind cranberries and oranges. Dissolve strawberry gelatin in hot water. Combine with remaining ingredients. Chill in mold or rectangular pan. The yield is 6 to 8 servings.

PEA RIDGE SNOW PEA SALAD

One 7 ounce package frozen
   Chinese snow peas or fresh
   peas
1 small head cauliflower

One 8 ounce can water
   chestnuts
2 tablespoons chopped pimento

DRESSING:
2 tablespoons sesame seed
⅓ cup vegetable oil
1 tablespoon lemon juice
1 tablespoon vinegar

1 tablespoon sugar
½ clove garlic, minced or 1/16
   teaspoon garlic powder
¾ teaspoon salt

Cook Chinese peas in one-half cup boiling water until slightly tender, but still crisp, about one minute after water boils. You can use fresh snow peas if you desire. Drain immediately after cooking to prevent overcooking. Separate cauliflower into flowerettes (about 2 cups). Cook in boiling, salted water about three minutes after water boils. Drain immediately. Combine peas, cauliflower, water chestnuts (sliced) and pimento. Chill.

To prepare dressing, place sesame seeds in shallow pan and bake at 350 degrees for five to eight minutes, until browned. Cool. In a covered jar, combine salad oil, lemon juice, vinegar, sugar, garlic, salt and sesame seeds. Chill. To serve salad, mix dressing throughly and add three tablespoons of dressing to vegetables. Toss lightly. The yield is 6 servings.

PINE BLUFF PINEAPPLE CREAM CHEESE SALAD

One 3 ounce package lemon
   gelatin
Two 3 ounce packages cream
   cheese
½ pint whipping cream,
   whipped or 2 cups non dairy
   topping

1 medium can crushed
   pineapple
½ - 1 cup pecans (chopped)

Prepare gelatin per package directions, using juice from pineapple as second cup water. Set in refrigerator to chill until soupy, not firm. Meanwhile, whip cream adding cream cheese gradually, until smooth and fluffy. Whip gelatin gradually adding cream and cheese mixture. Add pineapple and nuts. Set in refrigerator until firm.

PINEAPPLE GELATIN SALAD

One 3 ounce package
   gelatin—lemon, orange, or
   pineapple
1 cup boiling water

1 can crushed pineapple
1 cup cottage cheese
¼ cup chopped nuts

Disslove gelatin in boiling water. Drain pineapple, saving syrup and adding enough water with the syrup to make one cup of liquid. Add to gelatin and water. Chill until very thick. Add cheese, pineapple, and nuts.

"Fix yore own plate!"

PLATE FILLING SPINACH SALAD

1 large bunch fresh spinach
   leaves
2 boiled eggs, chopped
6 to 8 slices bacon, fried and
   crumbled

6 to 8 small green onions,
   chopped
Avocado slices, optional
Parmesan cheese
Italian dressing

Place spinach leaves on each plate. Sprinkle eggs, onions, and bacon over each spinach salad. Add avocado slices. Sprinkle with Parmesan cheese. Top with Italian dressing. The yield is 4 servings.

RASPBERRY COCKTAIL SALAD

1 can fruit cocktail, drained
1 can pineapple chunks
  (drained)
One 8 ounce package raspberry
  gelatin

One 8 ounce carton sour cream
3 cups non dairy whipped
  topping

Sprinkle the package of raspberry gelatin on the drained fruit, and let stand 30 minutes. Then add one carton of sour cream and topping. Mix well and let set in the refrigerator for several hours. The yield is 12 servings.

RED RIVER STRAWBERRY SALAD

Two 3 ounce packages
  strawberry gelatin
1 cup boiling water
Two 10 ounce packages frozen
  sliced strawberries (thaw, but
  do not drain)
1 large can crushed pineapple
  (drained)

3 ripe medium bananas
  (mashed)
1 cup chopped pecans
Two 8 ounce cartons sour
  cream

In large bowl, combine gelatin and boiling water. Remove from heat and fold in all ingredients except for sour cream. Pour half of the mixture into a pyrex dish and chill until firm. Spread sour cream over this and add remaining strawberry mixture and chill again until firm. The yield is 8 to 10 servings.

RICE SURPRISE SALAD

2 cups cooked rice
½ cup sugar
1 cup chopped apples
1 cup drained crushed
  pineapple
18 large marshmallows

½ cup chopped maraschino
  cherries
1 cup chopped pecans
2 cups non-dairy whipped
  topping

Cook rice to package directions. While rice is still warm add sugar and fold in marshmallows, apples, and pineapple. Refrigerate for 1 hour. Fold in whipped topping, cherries and pecans. Sprinkle top with nutmeg. Make 24 hours before serving time.

SIMPLE AGGIE AVOCADO

1 large avocado
1 dozen shrimp, cooked, peeled, and deveined

Remoulade sauce
1 tablespoon lemon juice

Peel avocado and slice it in half. Remove the seed. Brush lightly with lemon juice to prevent discoloration. Stuff each half with shrimp. Cover each with Remoulade sauce. Serve on a bed of lettuce. Simple enough for an Aggie! The yield is 2 servings.

VAN BUREN VEGETABLE SALAD

6 cups shredded lettuce
5 boiled eggs, sliced
One 16 ounce can tender green peas
1 pound bacon, fried, drained and crumbled

2 cups shredded Swiss or Cheddar cheese
¼ cup chopped green onions
1 cup mayonnaise
Paprika for garnish

Place ingredients in layers in a large salad bowl. Cover with cellophane wrap. Refrigerate for 24 hours before serving. This can be tossed before serving but is not necessary. The yield is 6 servings.

BLUE MOUNTAIN BLUE CHEESE SALAD DRESSING

1 cup sour cream
½ teaspoon dry mustard
½ teaspoon pepper
½ teaspoon salt
¼ teaspoon garlic powder

1 teaspoon Worcestershire sauce
1½ cups mayonnaise
4 to 6 ounces blue cheese

Blend all ingredients except blue cheese. Stir in crumbled cheese. This is better if made in advance and refrigerated for at least 24 hours before serving. The yield is 2½ cups.

POPPY SEED DRESSING

¾ cup sugar
1 teaspoon dry mustard
1 teaspoon salt
⅓ cup tarragon or white vinegar

1 tablespoon finely grated
  onion
1 cup vegetable oil
1½ tablespoons poppy seed

Mix all dry ingredients. Add vinegar and stir until dissolved. Slowly beat in oil until thick. Add onion and poppy seed. Great over fresh fruit salad of your choice. Easy to make in your blender or food processor.

RUBY'S MAYONNAISE

¼ cup vegetable oil
1 tablespoon vinegar
1 tablespoon lemon juice
1 egg
½ teaspoon salt

⅛ teaspoon paprika
¼ teaspoon dry mustard
¾ cup vegetable oil
Dash of cayenne

Combine above ingredients (except ¾ cup vegetable oil) in blender in order listed. Cover, blend 5 to 10 seconds without turning off blender. Remove cover and pour in ¾ cup of oil in a heavy stream. Blend 5 or 6 seconds more.

UNMISTAKABLY THE BEST SALAD DRESSING

1 cup mayonnaise
1 cup salad dressing
1¼ teaspoons paprika
¼ teaspoon monosodium
  glutamate

1 tablespoon lemon juice
1 tablespoon white vinegar
1 tablespoon sugar
⅓ cup of evaporated milk

Blend everything until smoothly textured. Serve on fresh crisp lettuce.

"Are you counting calories?"

Tips for dieting

- Before beginning a diet check with your physician.

- Drink an eight ounce glass of water before each meal.

- Snack on vegetables instead of sweets and salty items.

- Increase your activity or exercise.

- Avoid starches, cream, and sugar.

- Use seasonings instead of salt.

- Sauté foods in chicken or beef bouillon instead of oil.

- Substitute yogurt for sour cream.

- Cook pasta until soft. It will have ¼ less calories.

- Cook meats under broiler using a rack so the fat drips off.

- Never shop for groceries on an empty stomach.

- Avoid tasting as you cook.

- Eat slower and savor each bite.

- Eat only in a designated place.

- Never eat in front of the T.V.

- Be consistent!

APPETIZERS AND HORS D'OEUVRES

Artichoke, Arkadelphia Artichoke
Hors d'oeuvres 9
Cheese, Fried 9
Cheese Ball, Garlic 9
Cheese Ball, "Play Ball" 10
Cheese Puffs, Aunt Olive's 10
Dip, Eight Layered Party 11
Dip, Hot Artichoke 11
Dip, Hot Broccoli 11
Dip, Smackover Shrimp 12
Dip, Goal Post Shrimp 13
Dip, Tomato 13
Dip, Vegetable Patch 13
Ducks, Wild Duck Dewitt 14
Grapes, Mountainburg Frosted 14
Ham Puffs, Devil's Den 14
Mushrooms, Lemon 15
Mushrooms, Magnolia Marinated
Mushrooms, Shrimp, and
Artichokes 16
Mushrooms, Stuffed Hors d'oeuvres . . 16
Oyster, Hors d'oeuvres 16

BEVERAGES

Brandy Ice, Brinkley's 19
Cocoa-Mocha, Cosy 19
Colada, Crystal Springs 20
Green Lizard from Wilson 20
Mimosas, Mama's 21
Punch, Gelatine 21
Punch, Fruit Punch for a Crowd 21
Punch, L.C.'s Milk 22
Punch, Christmas Wassail 22
Slush, Pop's Soda Pop 23
Tea, Red Hot Razorback 23
Tea, Holiday Spiced 23
Yellow Bird, Yellville's 24

BREADS

Biscuit Mix, Cathead 27
Biscuits, Daybreak 28
Biscuit Wedges, Raisin 28
Bread, Pumpkin Patch 29
Buns, Hot Cross 29
Corn Bread, Home Town 30
Doughnuts, Fattening French 31
Loaf, Southern Sweet Dough
Cinnamon 31
Muffins, Blueberry Oatmeal 32
Muffins, Peanut Butter Corn Flake . . . 32
Muffins, Home Town Peanut Butter . . . 32
Pancakes, Blueberry Bear 33
Popovers, Button Poppin 33
Rolls, 15 Minute Dinner 33
Rolls, Quick Hour and a Half Dinner . . 34
Rolls, Southern Sweet
Dough Cinnamon 34
Rolls, Sunday Mornin Cinnamon 35

Southern Sweet Dough 35
Toast, Fancy French 36
Toast, Simple French 36
Spoon Bread, Appleton 37
Spoon Bread, Springdale 37

CAKES AND FROSTINGS

Angelfood Cake, Heavenly Angelfood
Cake and Fluffy Pineapple
Frosting 41
Angelfood, Surprise Loaf 41
Banana Split Cake, Tex-ark-ana 42
Carrot Cake, First Prize 42
Cheesecake, Dairy Delight 43
Cheesecake, Myrene's No Bake 43
Chocolate Cake, Big Flat Cola 44
Chocolate Cake, Big Fork
Buttermilk 44
Chocolate Cake, Mountain Home
Cinnamon 45
Choir Cake 45
Fig Cake, Toadie's Favorite 46
Fruitcake, Grandmother Duke's
White 47
Fruitcake, No Bake 47
Hallelujah Cake 48
Jam Cake, Ozark Mountain 49
Maxine's Hummingbird Cake 50
Pound Cake, Bodcaw Brown Sugar . . 50
Pound Cake, Greg's Fudge Center . . . 50
Prune Cake, Prize Winning 51
Pudding Cake, Mount Ida's Coconut
Lemon 51
Shortcake, Down Home 52
Sourcream Cake, Coconut 52
Strawberry Patch Cake 53
Sugar Cane Cake, Canehill 54
Vanilla Wafer Cake, Vicey's 54
Whitehall Whitecake with
Chocolate Curls 55
Whitehall Whitecake Chocolate
Filling 55
Bertha's Brown Sugar Icing 55
Caramel Frosting, Ozark 56
Chocolate Frosting, Gloria's
Two Minute 56
Lemon Cream Frosting, Jennifer's . . . 56
Seven Minute Frosting, Best Ever 57

CANDIES AND COOKIES

CANDIES

Brittle, Flaudie's Peanut 61
Brittle, Fresh Cracked Pecan 61
Datenut Balls, Saturday Night 61
Fudge, Lip Smacking Peanut Butter . . 62
Orange Balls, Southern 62
Toffee, Georgeanna's English 62
Washington's Favorite Candy 63

COOKIES

Brownies, I Just Love Those 63
Butter Cookies, Buddy Bear's 64
Grandma's Tea Cakes 64
Italian Cookies, Ella May's 64
Macaroons, McLarty's 65
Molasses Crinkles 65
Oatmeal, Old Fashioned Molasses . . . 66
Oatmeal, Oakhill No Bake 66
Oatmeal, Crispy Butterscotch 67
Peanut Butter, Picnic 67
Pollyanna 67
Sugar, Charlotte's Lemonade 68
Thumbprint, Timothy's 68

FISH AND SEAFOOD

Bass Delight, DeGray 71
Crab Newburg 71
Crab, Hot Crab Sandwich au
    "Pulaski" 72
Croquettes, Spring River Salmon 72
Deep South Deep Sea Casserole 73
Fish Fillets, Millwood Broiled 73
Flounder (Baked), Samantha's 74
Flounder, Vegetable Dinner 74
Fried Frog Legs, Jumpin 75
Lobster, Broiled Lobster Tails
    DeQueen 75
Lobster, Hollering Boiled Live 75
Out of the Ordinary Seafood
    Casserole 76
Red Snapper, Alma's 77
Seafood Imperial 77
Shrimp, Barbecued Little Rock 78
Shrimp Creole, Lafayette 78
Shrimp Gumbo, Quick 78
Shrimp, Stuttgart Rice and
    Shrimp Cantonese 79
Sole, Pan Fried "Dover" 79
Trout Almandine, Batesville
    White River 80
Trout, Norfork Lake 80

FOWL AND POULTRY

Chicken, A La Crema 83
Chicken, Alma's Chicken Breasts
    in Wine 83
Chicken, Aunt Busby's Sweet and
    Sour Chicken Fingers 83
Chicken, Bartholomew Lemon
    Baked 84
Chicken, Beebe's Lemon-Marinade
    Chicken Barbecue 84
Chicken, Chicken in Magnolia
    Mushroom Sauce 85
Chicken, Cream Cheese Chicken
    Dardanelle 85
Chicken, Evening Shade Chicken
    in Wine Sauce 86

Chicken, Home Sweet Home Chicken
    Breasts 86
Chicken, Little Flock Chicken
    Supreme 87
Chicken, Little Italy Chicken
    Cacciatore 87
Chicken, Nashville Baked Chicken
    with Peaches 88
Chicken, Pike County Sweet and
    Sour Baked 88
Chicken, Prairie Grove Smothered . . . 89
Chicken, Queen Wilhelmina Chicken
    Loaf 89
Chicken, Smothered Chicken with
    Mushroom Gravy 90
Chicken, Springdale Chicken with
    Vegetables 90
Chicken, Spring Valley Lemon
    Flavored Chicken Salad 90
Chicken, Walnut Hill Chinese 91
Chicken, Woodberry Oven
    Barbecued 92
Cornish Hens, Calhoun County
    Cornish Hens with Wild Rice
    Stuffing 92
Dove, Birdtown Dove Casserole 93
Dove, Clarksville Dove Au Vin 93
Goose, Jo's Roast 94
Quail, Osceola Oven Baked 95
Turkey, Boone County Baked Turkey . . 95
Turkey, Dressing 95
Turkey, Giblet Gravy 96
Turkey, Country Roasted Turkey 96
Wild Duck, Lodge Corner Apricot
    Wild Duck 97
Wild Duck, Peckerwood Wild Duck
    in Red Wine Gravy 97

FRUITS AND VEGETABLES

FRUITS

Apples, Apple Annie's Baked 101
Cantaloupe, Cotton Plant Cantaloupe
    with Port wine 101
Curried Fruit, Farmington 101
Grapefruit Halves, Broiled 101
Green Tomatoes, Fried
    Home Grown 102

VEGETABLES

Asparagus Casserole Ashdown 102
Beets, Ellie Mae's Quick
    Pickled Beets 103
Bellpepper, French Fried Bell
    Pepper Rings 103
Beans, King's Baked Barbecue
    Beans 103
Broccoli and Cheese Casserole 104
Broccoli and Corn Casserole 104

Broccoli, Oriental 104
Carrots, Monticello Marinated 105
Corn, Cousin Shonna's Corn
   Souffle 105
Corn, Corning Fried 105
Corn, Ravenden Roasted 106
Eggplant, Hot Out the Oven
   Eggplant Casserole 106
Green Beans, Polynesian 107
Green Beans, Snappin Easy
   French Style 107
Harrisburg Hungarian Cucumbers . . . 107
Pea Ridge Casserole 107
Peas, Fresh Purple Hull Peas
   and Hog Jowl 108
Potatoes, Commander's 108
Potatoes, Granny's Creamed 108
Potatoes, Polk County Potato
   Casserole 109
Spinach, Fairfield Bay Spinach
   Oyster Casserole 109
Squash, Garden Squash
   Casserole 110
Squash, Greenland Acorn 110
Squash, Sour Cream and Sausage
   Squash Casserole 110
Squash, Sunrise Squash and
   Sausage Casserole 111
Summer Vegetable Casserole 111
Sweet Potato, Carol Anne's Sweet
   Potato Casserole 111
Sweet Potatoes in Orange Halves 112
Turnip Greens, Mississippi County
   Turnip Greens and Ham Hock 112
Yams, Yodeling 112

MEATS
   Beef, Bull Shoals Beef Burgers 115
   Beef, Cheesy Beef Rolls a la
     Carlisle 115
   Beef, Des Arc Pepper Steak 116
   Beef, Glenda's Flank Steak
     Marinade 116
   Beef, Hamburg Goulash 117
   Beef, Mama Speck's Tufoli 118
   Beef, Meatballs in Mushroom
     Sauce 119
   Beef, Perfect Roast 119
   Beef, Roger's Mother's
     Smothered Liver 119
   Beef, Stuffed Pepper Devalls 120
   Beef, Sherwood English Prime Rib . . . 120
   Beef, Spanish Beef 121
   Beef, Steak Diane 121
   Beef, Sweden Pot Roast 122
   Beef, Vilonia Veal Parmesan 122
   Pork, Booneville Barbecued
     Pork Roast 123
   Pork, Culpepper Pork Chops 124

Pork, Cranberry Pineapple Chops 125
Pork, Marvell Glazed Pork Chops 126
Pork, Morrilton Mincemeat Stuffed . . . 126
Pork, Piggot Pork Chops and
   Arkansas Grown Rice 127
Lamb, Lita's Barbecued Leg
   of Lamb 127

MISCELLANEOUS—EGGS
   Eggs, Benedict 131
   Eggs, East Texas 131
   Eggs, Farmhouse, Bacon, Grits
     and Eggs 131
   Eggs, Garden Fresh Zucchini
     Quiche 132
   Eggs, Springdale Cheddar
     Scrambled 132
   Eggs, Quick Quiche 132

MISCELLANEOUS—OTHER DESSERTS
   Berdie B.'s Bread Pudding 133
   Cherry Valley Ice Cream 133
   Cream De Menthe Parfait 134
   Down Home Custard Ice Cream 134
   Homemade Chocolate Ice Cream 135
   Rasberry Lemon Souffle 135
   Soda Pop Ice Cream 136
   Tiny Gelatin Squares 136

MISCELLANEOUS—PICKLES
AND RELISHES
   Bertha's Bread and Butter Pickles 137
   Bradley County Green Tomato
     Relish 137
   Charleston Chutney 138
   Garland Garlic Pickles 138
   Hayden's Relish 138

MISCELLANEOUS—PRESERVES
   Peach Orchard Marmalade 139

MISCELLANEOUS—SAUCES
AND SPREADS
   Frenchman's Bayou Remoulade
     Sauce 139
   Fresh Butter Hollandaise Sauce 140
   Garlic Butter Sauce 140
   Speck's Marchand De Vin 140
   Strawberry Butter 141
   Summer Tomato Sauce 141
   Tarter Sauce 141
   White Sauce 142

MISCELLANEOUS—SNACKS
   Crispy Granola 142
   Nachos 142

PASTRIES AND PIES
   Apple Crisp, Johnny 145

Apple Squares, Washington 146
Cream Puffs, Sweet Home Tiny
    Chocolate Glazed 147
Cream Puff, Filling 147
Chocolate Glaze for Cream Puffs 147
Pie, Hamburg Fresh Strawberry 148
Pie, Hemitage Strawberry Parfait 148
Pie, Becky Jo's Sweethome Potato . . . 148
Pie, Black Rock Bottom 149
Pie Delightful Pecan 150
Pie, Frenchport Coconut 150
Pie, Old Jenny Lind Banana
    Almond 151
Pie, Peach Orchard Cream 151
Pie, Pickens Peach Parfait 152
Pie, Pineapple Supreme 152
Pie, Poor Man's Pecan 153
Pie, Rosebud Raisin 153
Pie Crust, Crumblin Graham
    Cracker 153
Pie Crust, Daisey's Cookie 154
Pie Crust, Prattsville Perfect 154
Tart, Lemon Blueberry 154

PENNY PINCHIN ONE DISH MEALS

Beef Potato Pie, Tuckerman 157
Chicken Casserole, Chickalah 157
Chicken and Broccoli Casserole,
    Camden 158
Chicken and Dumplings, Miller
    County Country 158
Chicken Waldo with White Rice 159
Chicken Spaghetti, Water
    Chestnut 159
Chicken Salad Casserole,
    Wooley Hollow 160
Chili Eldorado, Pork and Beans 160
Lasagna, Antoine 161
Macaroni and Cheese, Mr. Mac's 161
Mock Ravioli, Monticello 162
Rice Mushroom Casserole, Anna's . . . 162
Rice, Grand Prairie 162
Soup, Bud's Crab Bisque 163
Soup, Ham Bone Soup 164
Soup, Merry's Bean Soup 164
Soup, Mineral Springs Minestrone . . . 165
Soup, Romance Crab 165
Soup, Ozark Vegetable 166

Spaghetti, Suzanna's 167
Spaghetti, Jonesboro 167
Spaghetti, Mom's Best Chicken 168
Spaghetti, Plain ol' Italian 168
Spaghetti, Pork Ribs Spaghetti
    with Gravelly Gravy 169
Spaghetti Sauce with J. Benten
    Meatballs 170
Stew, Best Ever Beef Stew 170
Stew, Longhorn Fan Stew 171
Stew, Luxora Cabbage Stew 172
Stroganoff, Lockesburg Beef 172

SALADS AND SALAD DRESSINGS

Salad, Antioch Apricot Gelatin 175
Salad, Bald Knob Potato 175
Salad, Berryville Cranberry 176
Salad, Bibb 176
Salad, Cherry Hill Cola 176
Salad, Cherry Valley Gelatin 177
Salad, Christmas 177
Salad, Crittenden Cabbage Slaw 178
Salad, Greenland 178
Salad, Homestyle Fruit 179
Salad, Mandarin Orange
    Gelatine Salad 179
Salad, Mariana Spinach 179
Salad, Marshmallow 180
Salad, Orange, Pineapple,
    Cranberry 180
Salad, Pea Ridge Snow Pea 181
Salad, Pine Bluff Pineapple
    Cream Cheese 181
Salad, Pineapple Gelatin 182
Salad, Plate Filling Spinach 182
Salad, Rasberry Cocktail 183
Salad, Red River Strawberry 183
Salad, Rice Surprise 183
Salad, Simple Avacado 184
Salad, Van Buren Vegetable 184
Salad Dressing, Blue Mountain
    Blue Cheese 184
Salad Dressing, Poppy Seed 185
Salad Dressing, Ruby's
    Mayonnaise 185
Salad Dressing, Unmistakably
    the Best 185

Razorback Country Cooking
P. O. Box 1371
Texarkana, Arkansas 75504

Please send me ____ copies of **Razorback Country Cooking** at $10.95 per copy, plus $1.50 for postage and handling per book. Texas residents add 5.125% or .56¢ sales tax. Enclosed you will find my check or money order for $_____.

Name _____

Address _____

City _____ State _____ Zip _____

Razorback Country Cooking
P. O. Box 1371
Texarkana, Arkansas 75504

Please send me ____ copies of **Razorback Country Cooking** at $10.95 per copy, plus $1.50 for postage and handling per book. Texas residents add 5.125% or .56¢ sales tax. Enclosed you will find my check or money order for $_____.

Name _____

Address _____

City _____ State _____ Zip _____

Razorback Country Cooking
P. O. Box 1371
Texarkana, Arkansas 75504

Please send me ____ copies of **Razorback Country Cooking** at $10.95 per copy, plus $1.50 for postage and handling per book. Texas residents add 5.125% or .56¢ sales tax. Enclosed you will find my check or money order for $_____.

Name _____

Address _____

City _____ State _____ Zip _____

Reorder Additional Copies